Accent on Science

Authors

Dr. Robert B. Sund
University of Northern Colorado
Dr. Donald K. Adams
University of Northern Colorado
Dr. Jay K. Hackett
University of Northern Colorado
Dr. Richard H. Moyer
University of Michigan–Dearborn

Charles E. Merrill Publishing Co.
A Bell and Howell Company
Columbus, Ohio
Toronto, London, Sydney

Consultants

Content Consultants
Jeanne Bishop, Parkside Junior High, Westlake, OH
York Clamann, Abilene Ind. School District, Abilene, TX
Lucy Daniel, Rutherfordton-Spindale High School, Rutherfordton, NC
Annette Saturnelli, Marlboro Schools, Marlboro, NY
Robert Smoot, McDonogh School, McDonogh, MD
Reading Consultant
Richard Rezba, Virginia Commonwealth University, Richmond, VA
Safety Consultant
Franklin D. Kizer, Council of State Science Supervisors, Lancaster, VA
Special Needs Consultant
Janet Mansfield Davies, Boulder, CO

A Merrill Science Program

Accent on Science, Pupils' Editions, K–6, and Teachers' Editions, K–6
Accent on Science, Poster Cards, K
Accent on Science, Evaluation and Activity Programs (Spirit Duplicating Masters), 1–6
Accent on Science, Activity Books, 1–6, and Teachers' Annotated Editions, 1–6
Accent on Science, Teacher Resource Book

Authors

Dr. Robert B. Sund was Professor of Science Education at the University of Northern Colorado. A well-known educator, Dr. Sund's teaching experience spanned the elementary through college levels. He served as a department head and as a consultant to many school districts as well as many professional science and mathematics teachers' organizations. As author or coauthor of over twenty professional books including *Teaching Science Through Discovery, Teaching Modern Science, Creative Questioning and Sensitive Listening Techniques,* and *Piaget for Educators,* he is recognized internationally.

Dr. Donald K. Adams is Professor of Education and Area Coordinator, Education Field Experiences at the University of Northern Colorado. He holds a B.S. in Liberal Arts Social Science, an M.S. in Biological Science, and an Ed.D in Science Education with support in Earth Science. He has been instrumental in implementing personalized science and outdoor education programs for students in kindergarten through college. In his 24 years of teaching, he has served as a consultant to teacher preparation programs and science programs throughout the United States, Australia, and New Zealand.

Dr. Jay K. Hackett is Professor of Earth Science and Science Education at the University of Northern Colorado. He holds a B.S. in General Science, an M.S. in Chemistry and Physics, and an Ed.D in Science Education with support in Earth Science. A resource teacher for elementary schools, he conducts numerous workshops and professional talks. In his 20 years of teaching experience, he has taught and consulted on science programs from the elementary to the college level and remains active in local, state, and national science professional organizations.

Dr. Richard H. Moyer is Associate Professor of Education at the University of Michigan–Dearborn. He holds a B.S. in Chemistry and Physics Education, an M.S. in Curriculum and Instruction, and an Ed.D in Science Education. His 11 years of teaching experience includes all levels and currently involves teacher training and environmental education. He conducts numerous workshops and inservice training programs for science teachers and has authored an environmental attitude assessment instrument that has been used extensively for research purposes.

Reviewers: Teachers and Administrators
Glenda Bartlett, Sequoyah Elementary School, Russellville, AR
Sandra Eliason, Country Side Elementary School, Edina, MN
Phyllis Enger, Sunset Intermediate School, Seattle, WA
Carol Farland, Nashua School District, Nashua, NH
Frank Mondi, Margate Middle School, Margarte, FL
Edward Ortleb, St. Louis Public Schools, St. Louis, MO
Jacqueline Venenga, Hansen Elementary School, Cedar Falls, IA

Cover Photo: White waterlilies and cypresses in the Okefenokee Swamp by Wendall Metzen

Series Editor: Terry B. Flohr; **Project Editor:** Karen S. Allen; **Editors:** Janet Helenthal, Angelyn M. Horne, Susan A. Stasiak, Michele J. Wigginton; **Book Design:** William Walker; **Project Artist:** Paul Helenthal; **Artist:** David L. Gossell; **Illustrators:** Frank Fretz, April Gutheil; **Photo Editor:** Linda Hoffines; **Production Editor:** Annette Hoffman; **Paper Sculpture:** Roma Dalton

ISBN 0-675-07621-8

Published by

Charles E. Merrill Publishing Company
A Bell & Howell Company

Columbus, Ohio 43216

Table of Contents

To the Student

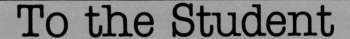

Science is all around you. It is part of your life. As you study ACCENT ON SCIENCE, you will learn much about yourself and your world.

You will look for answers to many questions. How are plants and animals alike? How are they different? What are machines? How are rocks formed? Why does the moon seem to change shape?

I will be your guide in this exciting study. We will explore many new ideas. Turn the page and let us begin.

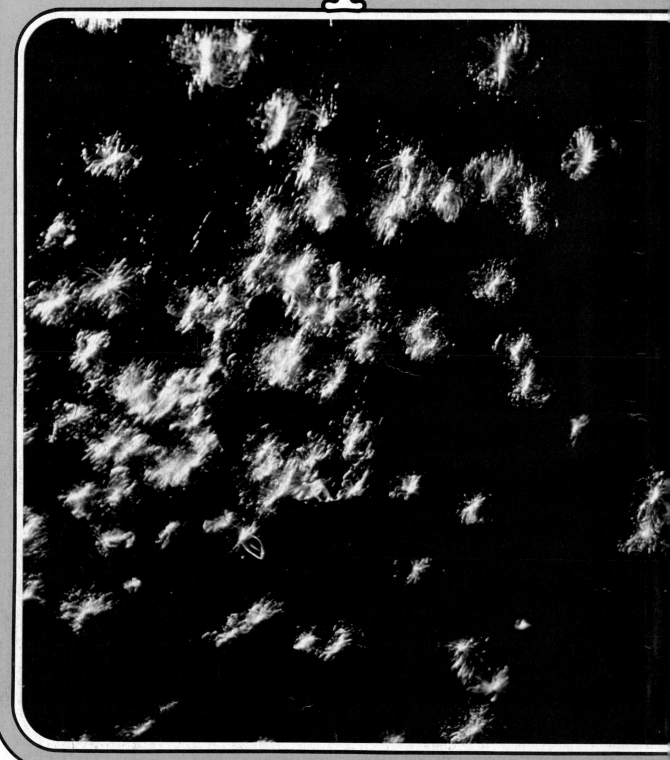

Seeds and Plants

Chapter One

Plant Beginnings

What are seeds? Where are seeds found?
What grows from seeds?

Suppose your teacher puts these objects on your desk. The class is asked to put the objects into two groups. How would you group the objects? The class groups the objects as the picture on the right shows. What are all these objects?

Seeds

Seeds are many colors, shapes, and sizes. Some seeds are light in color. Other seeds are dark. Some seeds are very large. Other seeds are almost too small to be seen. Even though seeds may look different, they are alike in one way. Every **seed** is a tiny plant and stored food. What might happen to the plant in each of the seeds above?

Activity

What Is in a Seed?

What to use:

2 bean seeds   hand lens
metric ruler   paper towel
plastic glass   pencil and paper
water

What to do:

1. Observe how the seeds look and feel. Measure and record the sizes of the two bean seeds. Soak the seeds in a glass of water overnight.

2. Measure and record the sizes of the two seeds again. Observe how the seeds look and feel.

3. Carefully peel away the outside of one seed. Observe this outside part of the seed with a hand lens.

4. Divide the bean into two halves. Observe the halves with a hand lens.

5. Find the tiny plant in the seed. Observe the plant with a hand lens. Draw what you see.

What did you learn?

1. How did the seeds change after they were soaked?

2. How many parts did the seed have?
3. Where was the tiny plant in the seed?
4. What parts does the tiny plant have?

Using what you learned:

1. Why are some seeds soaked before they are planted?
2. What do you think the outside part of the seed does?
3. What do you think is in the two halves of the seed?

Parts of a Seed

You learned that a tiny plant is in every seed. The tiny plant inside the seed is called an **embryo** (EM bree oh). Look closely at this embryo. What parts of the new plant can you see?

Part of every seed is also stored food. The **stored food** of a seed is food for the embryo. The embryo needs food to grow. Compare the size of this embryo with the stored food. Why does the embryo need so much food?

A seed also has a tough skin called a **seed coat.** The seed coat protects the other parts of the seed. What might happen if a seed did not have a seed coat?

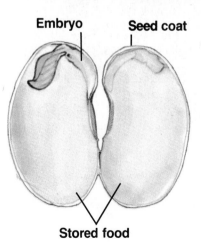

Embryo   Seed coat

Stored food

Activity

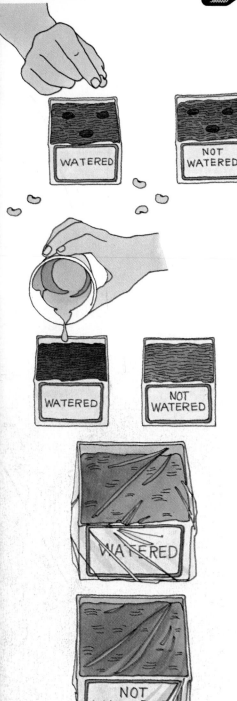

When Will Seeds Grow?

What to use:

2 small milk cartons
scissors
pencil and paper
labels
potting soil
6 soaked bean seeds

water
small paper cup
clear food wrap
foam meat tray
metric ruler

What to do:

1. Cut the tops off both milk cartons. Label the cartons **Watered** and **Not Watered.**

2. Fill each carton with soil. Gently pack the soil with your hands.

3. Use your finger to poke three holes in the soil of both cartons. Put one seed in each hole and cover the seeds with soil.

4. Add water until the soil is moist to the carton marked **Watered.**

5. Cover both cartons with plastic wrap. Put the cartons on a tray by the window.

6. Take the plastic wrap off both cartons after the seeds begin to grow. Water the soil only in the **Watered** carton.

7. Use the ruler to measure any plants that grow. Record their height every day for two weeks.

What did you learn?

1. What happened to the seeds?
2. How long did it take for young plants to appear?
3. In which carton were the tallest plants?

Using what you learned:

1. Suppose bean seeds were planted both in the desert and by a forest stream. Which seeds would probably grow?
2. What might happen if the seeds were planted in a place that had water and very cold temperatures?

When Seeds Germinate

Seeds germinate (JUR muh nayt) when they have what they need to grow. **Germinate** means the embryo starts growing from the seed. Most seeds do not germinate right after they form. Some seeds stay in the ground for a few months before germinating. Sometimes a seed may not germinate for many years.

A seed needs water to germinate. Water moves through the seed coat. The embryo begins to grow and the seed coat splits.

A warm temperature is also needed for a seed to germinate. Many seeds begin to grow in spring. The temperatures of the ground and air get warmer in spring.

Working with Trees

Who knows about trees? Forest rangers do. A forest ranger's job is to protect forests. Bill is a forest ranger. He does many things to protect the living things in the forests.

Bill spends part of his time deciding which trees can be cut down. He plants young seedlings to replace the old trees. He also tries to stop insects from harming the trees.

Part of his time is spent trying to stop forest fires. Some fires are started by lightning. Most fires are started by people. Large machines are used to stop the fires. Bill uses the machines to clear land in front of the fire. The fire cannot go across this cleared land. The fire dies out.

Forest rangers like to work outside. They like to work with people, too. They teach people how to take care of the forests. What can Bill teach you about forests? How can you help protect the forests?

Seedlings

After a seed germinates, the embryo grows into a young plant. The young plant is called a **seedling.** Seedlings need many things to keep growing. They need warm temperatures, water, and food.

Sometimes the temperatures early in spring get warm. The seeds germinate. The embryos grow into seedlings.

Seedlings also need the right amount of water. Too little water will cause the plants to die. Too much water can also kill some plants. When might a plant get too much water?

The embryo uses the stored food of a seed while it grows. This stored food lasts only a short time. Then, the seedling must make its own food. What do you think plants need to make their own food?

Activity

How Does Light Affect Plant Growth?

What to use:

3 small milk cartons
labels
pencil and paper
potting soil

9 bean seedlings
water
paper cup
2 tall boxes

What to do:

1. Label one milk carton **Light,** one carton **Some Light,** and one carton **No Light.**

2. Plant three seedlings in each carton. Add water to each carton until the soil is moist.

3. Place a tall box over the carton labeled **No Light.** Put the other two cartons near a window.

4. Every day at noon, place the second tall box over the carton labeled **Some Light.** Remove the box each morning.

5. Check the soil in each carton every other day. Add water if needed to make the soil moist.

6. After one week observe the plants in each carton. Record any changes you observe.

7. Wait a second week. Observe and record any changes.

What did you learn?

1. How did the seedlings in each carton look at the start of the activity?
2. How did the seedlings in each carton look after two weeks?
3. Which carton of seedlings grew the best?

Using what you learned:

1. Why do some kinds of plants live in sunny places and some live in shady places?
2. Why did you have to make sure that all three cartons were equally watered?

Plants need water and air to make their own food. Plants also need light to make food. Some plants need a lot of light. They grow where there is sunlight most of the time. Some plants do not need as much light. They grow in shady places. What might happen if plants that live in the shade were put in the sunlight?

Scattering Seeds

You know what seeds and seedlings need to grow. You also know that not all plants need the same amounts of water and light. Not all plants grow at the same temperature. Seeds grow in places that are at the right temperature and have the right amounts of water and light.

Most seed plants make many seeds. Some of the seeds fall under the plants. Not all of these seeds can grow. There is not enough room on the ground for all the new plants. Many seeds are scattered. **Scattered** means the seeds are moved to other places.

People scatter seeds when they plant them. Most foods we eat come from seeds planted by farmers. Many flowers and grasses grow from seeds planted in yards and parks. When have you planted seeds? How else have you scattered seeds?

Animals scatter seeds. Squirrels gather acorns and other seeds for food. They eat some of the seeds. They carry away other seeds and store them. Some of these seeds may drop on the ground. The squirrels may not find all of the seeds they stored. The dropped and lost seeds may germinate.

Birds scatter seeds. They eat some seeds. Other seeds may stick to their feet and feathers. These seeds may drop to the ground as the birds fly. When might the seeds germinate?

Other animals scatter seeds. Animals with fur scatter seeds that stick to their bodies. Which of the seeds below could stick to fur? Why?

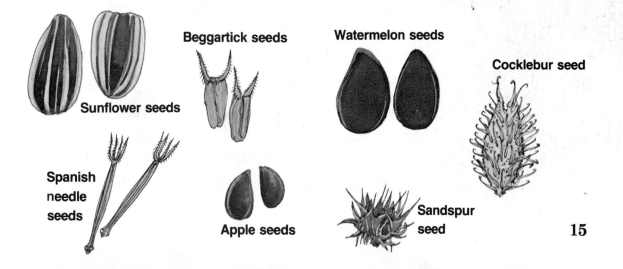

Sunflower seeds

Beggartick seeds

Watermelon seeds

Cocklebur seed

Spanish needle seeds

Apple seeds

Sandspur seed

15

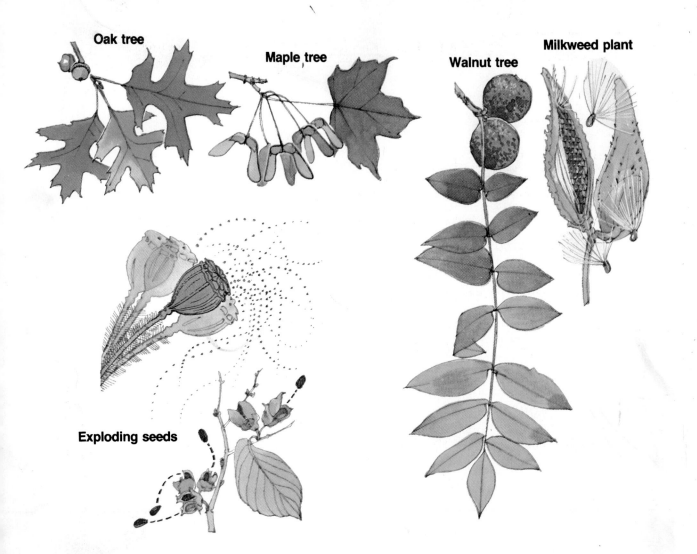

Oak tree

Maple tree

Walnut tree

Milkweed plant

Exploding seeds

The wind scatters seeds. Some seeds grow inside plant parts called **pods.** The pods get ripe and break open. Some of the seeds are blown away by the wind. Sometimes the seeds even shoot out of the pods. Look at the pictures above. Which seeds might drop to the ground? Which seeds might be scattered by the wind? How can you tell?

People, animals, and wind scatter seeds. How else can seeds be scattered?

16

Chapter Review

Summary

- A seed is a tiny plant and stored food.
- The plant inside a seed is an embryo.
- The embryo uses stored food when it grows.
- The seed coat protects the embryo and stored food.
- Seeds germinate when they have the right amount of water and are at the right temperature.
- Seedlings need warm temperatures and the right amounts of water and light to keep growing.
- People, animals, and wind scatter seeds.

Science Words

seed	germinate
embryo	seedling
stored food	scattered
seed coat	pods

Questions

1. What are the parts of a seed?
2. What do seeds need to germinate?
3. What do seedlings need to grow?
4. Why must some hard seed coats break open before they can germinate?
5. How are seeds scattered?
6. Why do people plant gardens in the spring?

Chapter Two
Plants
from Seeds

What kind of plants are shown here?
Why are there many kinds of plants? How
are all of these plants alike?

Plants are all around you. You see trees and bushes on the way to school. You eat fruits and vegetables. You may even wear cotton clothes. Many of the plants you see and use grow from seeds. Plants that grow from seeds are called **seed plants.**

Seed Plants Are Different

Not all seed plants look alike. Seed plants are different sizes and shapes. Trees can be large or small. A corn plant may be tall and thin. A rose bush may be short and bushy. How are the seed plants on the left different?

Not all seed plants grow in the same kinds of places. They may grow in wet or dry places. They may grow in sunny or shady places. They may grow in cold or hot places, too. Seed plants grow in large fields and small pots. Some grow between cracks in sidewalks and walls. Some seed plants even grow in water. Where can you find seed plants growing around you?

Parts of Seed Plants

You know that there are many different kinds of seed plants. Most of these different plants have the same kinds of parts. Some of the parts grow under the ground. The roots of most seed plants grow under the ground. Some of the parts grow above the ground. The stems, leaves, and flowers of most seed plants grow above the ground. Find these four plant parts below.

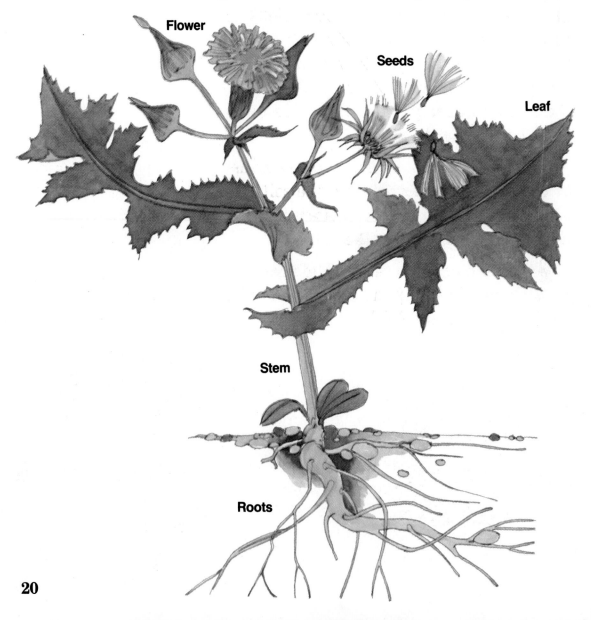

Flower

Seeds

Leaf

Stem

Roots

Roots

Roots are the plant parts that hold plants in the ground. You do not see the roots of most plants. Yet, the roots form almost half of the plant. Plants without roots may be easily blown or washed away.

Most roots can be put into two groups. Roots in one group are made of one main part. The main root is long and thick. It may grow deep into the ground. A carrot plant has a long, thick main root. Roots in the other group are made of many small roots. These roots look like branches or strings. They spread out and grow close to the surface of the ground. The grass in a lawn has stringlike roots.

Roots also absorb water. Absorb means to take in. Water moves from the soil into small "tubes" in the roots. Water moves up the tubes to the stem of the plant.

What kind of root does each of these plants have? Which plant might be harder to pull from the soil? Why?

Stems

Seed plants have stems. **Stems** hold up the other plant parts that are above the ground. Some plants have stems that are soft and green. Some plants have stems that are thick, hard, and not green. What kind of stem does a large tree have?

Stems also carry water. The small tubes from the roots go up through the stems. Water moves up from the roots, through the stems, and into the leaves. Other tubes in the stem carry food. Food in the tubes moves down from the leaves to the roots.

Plants may have more than one stem. Find the stems of these plants. How are the stems different? How are they alike?

Activity

Where Does the Water Go?

What to use:

small jar	eyedropper
water	spoon
blue food coloring	celery stalk with leaves

What to do:

1. Fill the jar half full of water. Add six drops of food coloring and stir.

2. Observe the celery. Place it in the colored water.

3. Observe the celery after two hours.

4. Take the celery out of the water. Your teacher will cut across the bottom and top of the celery.

5. Observe the cut ends of the celery.

What did you learn?

1. What did the ends of the celery look like in step 2 and in step 5?

2. What happened to the celery after two hours? How did the change happen?

Using what you learned:

1. Why do we put cut flowers in water?

2. Why does a flower wilt when its stem is broken?

Leaves

Most seed plants have green leaves. **Leaves** are the plant parts in which food is made. Some green leaves also store food. Air, water, and sunlight are used to make food in the leaves.

Tubes from the roots and stems go into the green leaves. In leaves, the small tubes are called veins. Why do you think the tubes are called veins? Water moves up through the tubes in the roots and stems into the veins of the leaves. What do you think moves down from the veins into the tubes of the roots and stems?

Look at the leaves above. The veins on each leaf form a different pattern. People use the pattern of the veins to tell different leaves apart.

Leaves can be put into groups. Some leaves look like needles. The needles may be long or short. Other leaves are broad and flat. Which leaves look like needles? Which leaves are broad and flat?

Broad leaves can also be put into groups. Some broad leaves have only one part. Leaves with one part are called **simple leaves.** Other broad leaves are made of several parts. These parts look like small leaves and are called **leaflets** (LEE flutz). Leaves made of leaflets are **compound leaves.** Where are the simple leaves? How many compound leaves are shown?

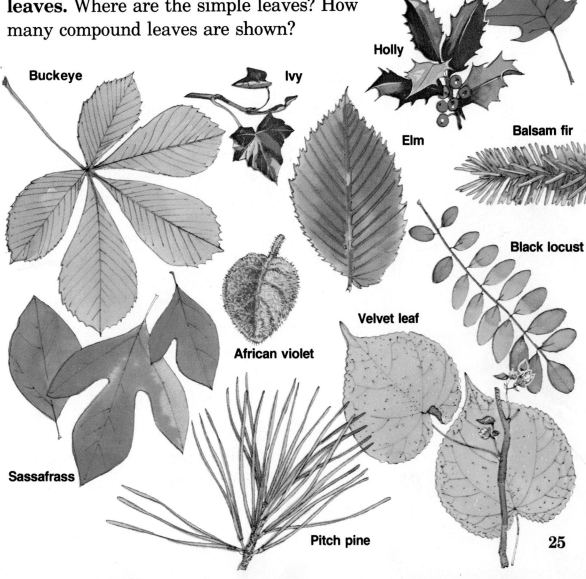

Ginkgo

Red oak

Holly

Buckeye

Ivy

Elm

Balsam fir

Black locust

Velvet leaf

African violet

Sassafrass

Pitch pine

25

Flowers and Cones

Some seed plants have flowers. A **flower** is the part of a plant in which seeds form. Most people think that all flowers have bright colors. Many flowers do not have bright colors. Some flowers may be green, pale yellow, or brown. Each picture above shows a different plant. Find the flowers on each plant. Tell how the flowers look.

Seeds form inside flowers. Sometimes many seeds form inside one flower. Sometimes only a few seeds form. How many seeds formed in the flower on the left? How do you think the seeds from this flower will be scattered?

Some seed plants do not have flowers. Seed plants that do not have flowers form seeds inside **cones.** Pine trees and fir trees are two kinds of seed plants that have cones instead of flowers.

Plant Cycle

Seed plants change. At first the seeds germinate. Then the seedlings grow into adult plants. The adult plants form seeds. Many kinds of plants form their seeds in flowers. Other kinds of plants form their seeds in cones. Seeds from both kinds of plants are scattered. They germinate and new plants grow. The same changes happen to the new plants, too. The germinating, growing, and forming of new seeds are parts of the **plant cycle.** The plant cycle happens over and over again.

Some kinds of plants germinate, grow, and form seeds in one year. Other kinds of plants take more than one year to go through these changes. No matter how many years are needed, all seed plants go through a plant cycle.

Plant Cycles

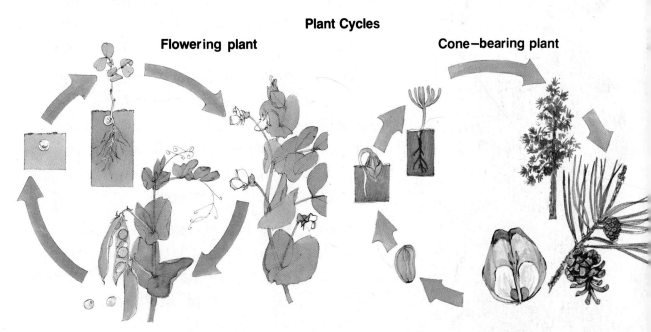

Flowering plant

Cone−bearing plant

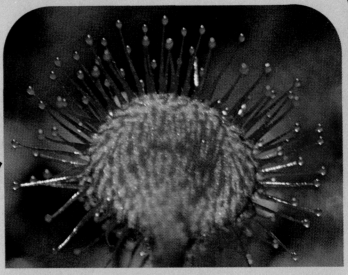

Watch Out for the Meat-Eaters

Why should ants stay away from these plants? These plants are meat-eaters. Most plants make their own food. Meat-eating plants live in places that have poor soil. They cannot make enough food. So, they trap and eat insects, spiders, and other small animals.

Sundews are one kind of meat-eater. They have a sticky liquid on their tips. Insects stick to the liquid. The tips curl over and hold the animal.

Venus's-flytraps are another meat-eater. The leaves of this plant close quickly to trap insects. The dead insect becomes food for the plant.

Pitcher plants have leaves shaped like a pitcher. Rainwater collects in the leaves. Insects fall into the water and die. The plant has a new meal to eat.

Chapter Review

Summary

- Seed plants have roots, stems, and leaves.
- Roots hold plants in the ground and absorb water.
- Stems hold up plants.
- Plants make food in their leaves.
- Water and food move through the plants in tubes.
- Seeds form in flowers or in cones.
- The germinating, growing, and forming of new seeds are the parts of the plant cycle.

Science Words

seed plants	leaflets
roots	compound leaves
stems	flower
leaves	cones
simple leaves	plant cycle

Questions

1. How does water in the soil get to all plant parts?
2. Choose one seed plant. Tell how it changes during its plant cycle.
3. What do roots of a plant do?
4. What does the stem of a plant do?
5. What happens in the green leaves of plants?
6. Why are flowers important to some kinds of seed plants?

Self Checks

Answer these Self Checks on a sheet of paper.
1. Draw a picture of a plant cycle. Label each part.
2. Draw a picture of the inside of a bean seed. Label each part.
3. What would happen if seeds were not scattered?
4. How do all plant parts get water?
5. How is a simple leaf different from a compound leaf?
6. Put the letters **a** through **h** on your paper. By each letter, write how the seed may be scattered.

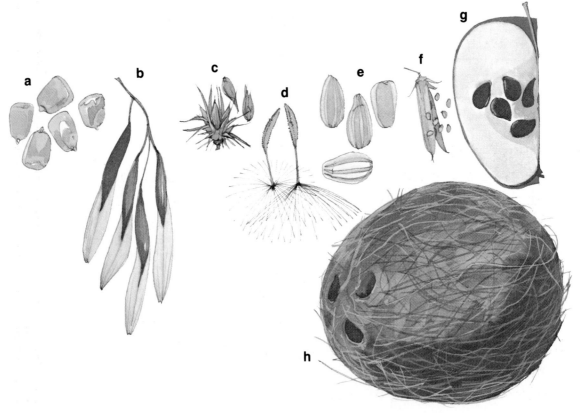

Idea Corner

More Fun with Science

1. Invent a seed that could be scattered by (a) the wind, (b) water, or (c) animals.
2. How many kinds of seeds do people eat? Find out as many as you can. Draw or write your report.
3. Make a map of North America or the world. Show where plants can be grown all year long.
4. Make a leaf collection. Group the leaves with the same kind of veins.
5. Grow some plants from seeds. Find out what each plant needs to grow best.

Reading for Fun

Eat the Fruit, Plant the Seed by Millicent E. Selsam, William Morrow Co.: New York, © 1980.
   Find out how to grow plants from the seeds of six different fruits.

Flowers of a Woodland Spring by Carol Lerner, William Morrow Co.: New York, © 1979.
   Study the life cycles and plant parts of wildflowers.

Sunflower by Martha McKeen Welch, Dodd, Mead, & Co.: New York, © 1980.
   Follow the life cycle of a sunflower.

Work and Machines

Chapter One

Forces and Work

What actions in the picture look like fun to you? What actions look like work? How can an action be both fun and work?

Harry and his sister Angie are buying food for tonight's dinner. The shopping list is very long. Harry and Angie cannot carry all the food. They need to use a shopping cart. How can they make the shopping cart move?

Push or Pull

Many objects will move if you push or pull them. A push or a pull is a **force.** These students are moving objects in their classroom. They are using forces. Which students are using pulling forces? Which students are using pushing forces?

An object will move when you lift it. Lifting is a force. Do you use a push or a pull to lift a chair off the floor?

Activity

How Much Pull Does It Take?

a

What to use:

cardboard strip   3 paper clips
strong rubber band   5 small objects
masking tape   pencil and paper
string (30 cm)

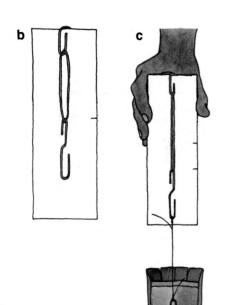
b   c

What to do:

1. Make a "Puller Pal" like the one shown.

2. Make a pencil mark to show where the rubber band ends.

3. Hook an object to your "Puller Pal." Lift the object as shown in the picture.

4. Make a pencil mark to show how far the rubber band stretches. Write the name of the object by the mark.

5. Repeat steps 3 and 4 with the other four objects.

What did you learn?

1. Which object took the most force to lift? How do you know?
2. Which object took the least force to lift?

Using what you learned:

1. Which takes more force, (a) to lift an object off the table, or (b) to pull the object across the table?
2. Find three small objects. Which object takes the largest force to lift?

How Much Force?

Pretend that you are going to clean your room. You have to lift many objects off the floor to put them away. Sometimes you use a large force to lift an object. Sometimes you use only a small force.

The amount of force needed to move an object depends on how much of that one object there is. While you are cleaning, you find two boxes. Both boxes are the same size. One is filled with rocks. One is filled with stamps. Which box takes more force to lift? Why? Which of the objects on the right would take a small force to lift?

Another Pulling Force

What happens to a kite when you pull on its string? Just as you pull on objects, the Earth pulls on objects, too! It even pulls on you. You can feel the pull when you jump up in the air. The pull between the Earth and other objects is a force called **gravity** (GRAV ut ee).

Gravity can move objects. When you jump up, gravity causes you to fall back to Earth. When you throw a ball, gravity pulls it back to Earth.

How is gravity causing the paint and flour to move? What would happen to them without gravity? How would your life change without gravity?

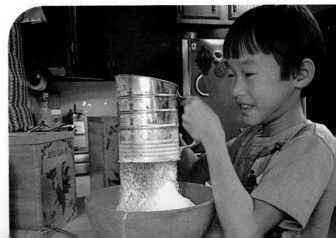

38

Work and Energy

You have learned that forces cause objects to move. Scientists say that **work** is done when a force moves an object. Where is work being done in the picture above? How do you know?

To find the amount of work done, you must first know how much force is needed to move an object. Some objects need more force than others to be moved. You must also know how far the object is moved. The amount of work done depends on both force and distance. More work is done if a wagon is pulled ten meters instead of five meters. In the picture, who is doing the most work? Why?

Look at these girls. They are helping their teacher return some books to a bookcase. The books move because the girls use a force. Which one is doing more work? Why? How could they both do the same amount of work?

A nail is forced into a board when hit by a hammer. Objects may move when they are pushed or pulled by a force. Each time a force moves an object, such as the books or a nail, work is done. When work is done, energy (EN ur jee) is used. **Energy** is the ability to do work. The girls can do work because they have energy. You are able to do work because you have energy, too. The more work you do, the more energy you use.

Chapter Review

Summary

- A push or a pull is a force.
- The amount of force needed to move an object depends on how much of the object there is.
- Gravity is the pull between the Earth and other objects.
- Work is done when a force moves an object.
- The amount of work done depends on both force and distance.
- Energy is the ability to do work.

Science Words

force   work
gravity   energy

Questions

1. Name three objects that you moved today. What kinds of forces did you use to move them?
2. Which will take more force to move,
   (a) a wooden block the size of a chalkboard eraser or
   (b) a wooden block the size of a shoe box?
3. Why are different amounts of force needed to move objects?
4. You and a friend carry flowerpots from the store to your house. All of the flowerpots are exactly alike. You carry two pots. Your friend carries one. Who does more work? How do you know?
5. How are energy and work related?

Chapter Two
Simple Machines

What is this person thinking? How would you solve the problem?

You have learned that a force may move an object. Work is done when the object moves. Sometimes a lot of force is needed to do work. What work did you do today that used a lot of force? These two students are moving bags. Which way would you want to move the bags? Why?

Pulley

Screw

Machines

Work can be made easier by using machines. People use machines to move objects. They use many kinds of machines. Machines with few or no moving parts are called **simple machines.** Each of these objects is a simple machine. How can each one make work easier?

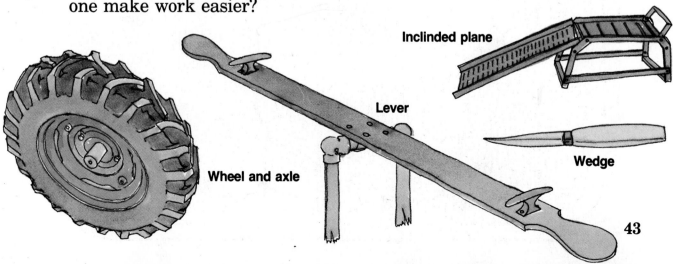

Inclinded plane

Lever

Wedge

Wheel and axle

43

Lever

These people are lifting objects. Which person is making work easier? The person on the left is using a lever. A **lever** is a simple machine which can be used to lift objects. What is the name of the lever the girl is using?

All levers use three parts. Any object to be lifted is called the **load.** The point where the lever rocks back and forth is called the **fulcrum.** A push or a pull that moves the lever is called the **force.** Find the load, fulcrum, and force in the picture.

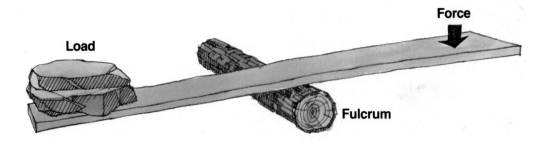

Load

Force

Fulcrum

Activity

How Much Push Does It Take?

What to use:

3 pencils

masking tape

metric ruler

small ball of clay

5 to 8 large metal washers

pencil and paper

What to do:

1. Tape the pencils together as shown and put them under the middle of the ruler.

2. Put the clay at one end of the ruler.

3. Add washers one at a time to the other end until the ball is lifted.

4. Record how many washers it took to lift the ball.

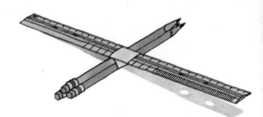

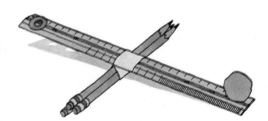

What did you learn?

1. What simple machine did you make?
2. What part of the machine was the force? What was the load?
3. How many washers lifted the load?

Using what you learned:

1. What happens to the force needed if you move the fulcrum? How can you find out?
2. Where do you put the fulcrum to use the smallest force? the largest force?

Suppose you and a friend are playing ball in the yard. A large rock is in your way. Your friend uses a board and log to set up a lever. The log is at the center of the board. Both of you push on the board to move the rock.

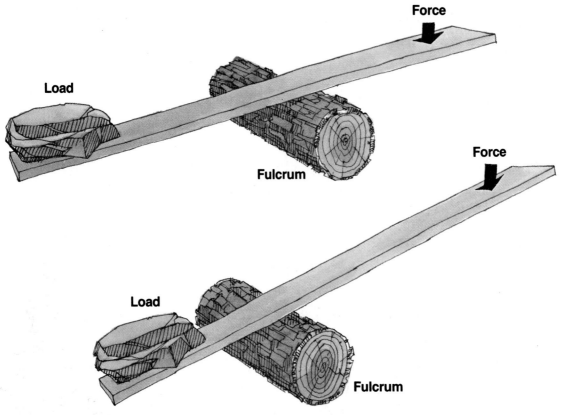

Later, you must move the rock by yourself. You set up the lever again. This time you put the log closer to the rock. What will happen when you push on the board? What will happen if you move the log further away from the rock and push?

The amount of force needed to lift a load changes with the position of the fulcrum. The closer the fulcrum is to the load, the easier the load can be lifted.

Not all levers are the same. Some levers do not have the fulcrum between the force and the load. The nutcracker is a lever with the fulcrum at one end. The force is at the other end. The load is in the middle.

Nutcracker

The picture shows a person doing work. This machine is a lever, too. Find the fulcrum of the lever. Find the force and the load. When do we use this machine? What is the name of this machine? Why do we call this machine a lever?

Activity

How Do Inclined Planes Make Work Easier?

What to use:

"Puller Pal" milk carton pencil
ramp (board) 8 books

What to do:

1. Lift the milk carton with the "Puller Pal." Mark how far the rubber band stretches.

2. Use four books. Set up the ramp, milk carton, and "Puller Pal" as shown.

3. Pull the carton up the ramp. Mark how far the rubber band stretches.

4. Put all eight books under the ramp.

5. Try the activity again. Mark how far the rubber band stretches.

What did you learn?

1. Which way took more force to move the milk carton?

2. Which way took less force?

Using what you learned:

1. Suppose you make the ramp higher. What will happen to the force needed?

2. Some roads go around a mountain instead of straight up its side. Why are the roads built around the mountain?

Inclined Plane

An **inclined plane** is a simple machine used to move objects to a higher place. A ramp is an inclined plane. A sidewalk going up a hill is an inclined plane, too. There may be inclined planes in your school. How are they used? Where else have you seen inclined planes?

Both boys want to go to the top of the hill. One path is shorter and steeper than the other. The boy on the steeper path goes a shorter distance. He uses much force to get to the top. The boy on the other path goes a longer distance. He uses less force to get to the top. The second boy can go up the hill easier than the first boy. The longer the distance moved on an inclined plane, the less force needed to go to the top.

A **wedge** (WEJ) is a simple machine made of two inclined planes. A force moves the wedge when work is done. Sometimes a wedge is used to raise objects a short distance. Sometimes a wedge is used to push objects apart. How can you use each wedge shown? What kind of force can move each wedge?

You know the force needed to raise an object with an inclined plane depends on the distance moved. A longer distance is covered when the inclined plane is wrapped around a post. A **screw** is an inclined plane that is wrapped around a post. Since a longer distance is covered, less force is used to turn a screw than to pound a nail into a piece of wood.

What screws do you see on this page? How are they used?

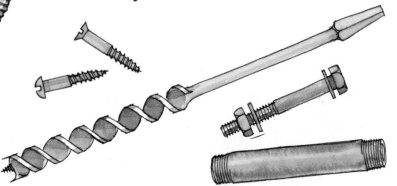

Wheel and Axle

Which door would you want to try to open? Why? The doorknob is a wheel and axle. A **wheel and axle** is a simple machine with a wheel that turns on a post. The post is called an axle.

Compare the sizes of the wheel and the axle in the picture. The distance around the wheel is greater than the distance around the axle. Less force is needed to turn the wheel than to turn the axle. Work is easier to do.

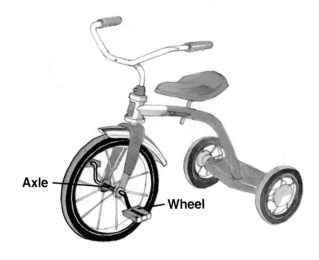

Axle —

Wheel

A wheel with teeth is called a **gear.** The teeth are made to fit together. When one gear turns, it can turn another gear. What kinds of machines have gears?

If you turn the red gear to the left, what happens to the green gear? Gears may be used to change direction of moving parts in machines. Drivers use gears in a car to go forward and to go backward.

Pretend that you are turning the red gear. Will the green gear turn faster or slower than the red gear? You turn the red gear one time. How many turns will the green gear make?

Clothesline

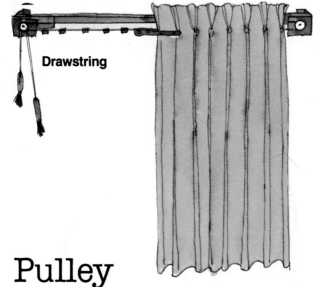
Drawstring

Flagpole

Pulley

A **pulley** is a simple machine used to lift heavy loads. It can also move objects to places that are hard to reach.

What type of force is used with these pulleys? Sometimes it is easier to pull on objects than to push on them. Sometimes less force is needed to lift the objects when a pulley is used.

Pulleys can also be used to change the direction of a force. Changing the direction of a force may make work easier to do. What happens to the load if you pull down on the flagpole rope? In which direction does each load move in the pictures above?

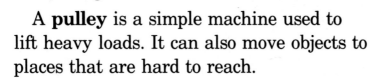

53

Building a Thrill Ride

What is the highest, fastest, and steepest ride you know? Most people will say a roller coaster. It only takes a few minutes to ride a roller coaster. It takes many months to build one.

Jack, Sally, and Mary build roller coasters. Jack is an engineer. He plans how steep each hill will be. He knows where to put each turn. He decides what shape the cars should be and how to attach them to the ride.

Mary is an artist. She uses Jack's plans to make drawings of the ride.

Her drawings show exactly what the ride will look like. Sally uses Jack's plans and Mary's drawings to make a model of the ride. Toy cars are added to the model. Sally makes sure the ride is safe by using the model. Then, the real ride is built. It is made of steel and plastic.

Jack, Mary, and Sally know when they have done a good job. People wait in long lines to ride the roller coaster. How do you feel when you ride a roller coaster?

■■■Chapter Review

Summary

- Simple machines have few or no moving parts.
- Levers, inclined planes, wedges, screws, wheels and axles, and pulleys are simple machines.
- Inclined planes are used to move objects to a higher place.
- Wedges and screws are two kinds of inclined planes.
- A wheel and axle is a wheel that turns on a post.
- Gears are wheels with teeth.
- Pulleys lift loads and change the direction of a force.

Science Words

simple machines	wedge
lever	screw
load	wheel and axle
fulcrum	gear
force	pulley
inclined plane	

Questions

1. Which simple machine are you using when you
   (a) put a hose on a faucet?   (c) cut an orange?
   (b) open a paint can?   (d) walk up a ramp?
2. What are the three parts of a lever?
3. Why is work easier to do using an inclined plane?
4. Give two reasons why you would use a pulley to lift an object.
5. What simple machine is formed by putting two inclined planes together?
6. What type of simple machine is a doorknob?

Chapter Three

Combining Machines

How is the machine below being used? How is the machine different from a simple machine?

A day at the county fair can be lots of fun. There are shows to see, rides to go on, and food to eat. Everywhere you look there are machines. Machines are used to make the food and set up the shows. Even the rides are machines.

Compound Machines

You have just learned about simple machines. Some simple machines have few moving parts. Some have no moving parts. However, most machines people use have many moving parts. Most machines are compound machines. A **compound machine** is made of two or more simple machines.

What compound machine do you see here? What simple machines can you find in the compound machine?

57

Activity

How Can You Use a Machine?

What to use:

foam meat tray
scissors
thick cardboard
  (3 × 6 cm)
rubber band
2 paper fasteners
masking tape

large pan filled
  with water
ruler
watch with second
  hand
pencil and paper
2 or 3 crayons

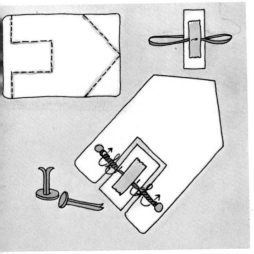

What to do:

1. Use the meat tray as your boat. Cut out the tray in the shape shown.

2. Tape the rubber band to both sides of the cardboard to make a paddle.

3. Put one paper fastener in each back section of the boat. Loop one end of the rubber band around each fastener.

4. Twist the rubber band around several times to wind up the paddle. Put your boat in the water at one end of the pan.

5. Record how far the boat moves. Record how many seconds the boat moves.

6. Tape a crayon to the top of the boat. Repeat steps 4 and 5.

7. Add more crayons. Repeat steps 4 and 5 again.

What did you learn?

1. What made your boat move?
2. What happened to the distance the boat moved as each crayon was added?

Using what you learned:

1. What could you do to make your boat move farther?
2. What could you do to make your boat move faster?

Machines for Transportation

How did you get to school today? If you rode in a bus or a car, you used a compound machine. People can use compound machines to move from place to place. Machines used to carry people and objects are kinds of **transportation.** Trucks, trains, boats, and planes are some kinds of transportation. How would your life change if there were no machines for transportation?

The First Flying Machine

Who flew a plane made of wood, cloth, and wire? The Wright brothers did. They were the first people to fly in a plane.

Wilbur and Orville named their first plane *The Flyer*. *The Flyer* was a biplane. Biplanes have two wings. Their plane was built of cotton cloth stretched over a wood frame.

Orville made the very first flight. It was not a comfortable ride. Orville laid on his stomach in the center of the plane. Wires were attached from his hips to the wings. He moved his hips to control the direction of the plane.

Orville's flight lasted 12 seconds. He flew only a short distance. His plane did not fly fast. A car goes much faster than this plane did.

Modern planes look very different from *The Flyer*. They are made of strong metals. They may hold more than a hundred people. They also fly very fast.

You can see *The Flyer* and other more modern planes. They are in a museum in Washington, D.C. How would you feel riding in a modern plane? How would you feel about riding in *The Flyer*?

People Using Machines

You have to buy a birthday gift. You find a shirt you like. The shirt comes in many colors and sizes. You wonder how so many shirts can be made.

Many items you buy are made in factories. A **factory** is a place that has many machines that make one type of object. A clothing factory has machines that cut and sew cloth. Other machines move the finished clothes to places where they are folded and put into boxes. Still other machines put the boxes in trucks.

People use machines for many reasons. Machines are used because they are fast. Machines may do a better job than people do. Machines also do jobs that are dangerous for people to do. Why do you think machines are used in these factories?

61

People use machines in factories and for transportation. People also use machines in growing food. What machines do farmers use? How are the farm machines used in growing food?

You use machines at home and at school. You use machines for work and for play. How are these machines being used?

Safety and Machines

Machines are helpful to us when we use them the right way. Machines can cause problems when they are not used the right way. Everyone who works with machines needs to know that accidents can happen if they use the machines carelessly.

Some machines make loud noises. People around loud noises for long periods of time may lose their hearing. Many people who work close to loud noises wear ear guards or ear plugs. List the machines you think make loud noises.

Some machines throw out sparks, pieces of wood, or other objects. People near these machines need to protect their eyes. What can they do to protect their eyes from flying objects?

What machines do you use that have sharp edges? What machines do you use that have fast moving parts? You may think that only adults use machines that can cause harm. Look around your school and your home. Many machines you use can cause harm if you are careless. How can you be sure to use these machines in safe ways? How are these people using machines in a safe way?

It is very important for people to use all machines safely. Learn all the safety rules BEFORE you use a machine. Discuss these rules with an adult before using the machine. Remember to follow the rules.

Chapter Review

Summary

- Compound machines are made of two or more simple machines.
- Machines can be used for transportation.
- Machines make many of the items we buy.
- Machines are fast and may do a better job than most people do.
- Machines are safe when people use them correctly.
- Always follow the safety rules when using machines.

Science Words

compound machine
transportation
factory

Questions

1. How are compound machines different from simple machines?
2. Name three compound machines. How are they used?
3. What machines are used in the kitchen?
4. What safety rules should be followed when using a bicycle?
5. How would a school day be different without compound machines?
6. Why are machines often used to paint cars in factories?
7. What machines are used to grow food?
8. How can you protect your ears from loud machines?

Self Checks

Answer these Self Checks on a sheet of paper.
1. Give an example of work you could do with each of these machines. Draw a picture of each machine.
   (a) lever   (c) pulley
   (b) inclined plane (d) wedge
2. Look around your classroom. Make a list of the machines you see. Tell whether they are simple or compound machines.
3. In which pictures is work being done? Why?
4. Write a safety rule for the use of each of these machines.
   (a) bicycle   (c) knife
   (b) saw   (d) lawn mower

Match the phrases in column A with the words in column B.

A	B
5. machine made of simple machines	fulcrum
6. wear ear guards when working with noisy machines	force
	screw
7. push or pull	gravity
8. the pull between the Earth and you	compound
9. an inclined plane wrapped around a post	machine
	safety rule
10. the point on which a lever rocks back and forth	

Idea Corner
More Fun with Science

1. Collect pictures from magazines that show the six simple machines. Classify the pictures and make a bulletin board.

2. Gather pictures that show people using machines for sports and games. Make a booklet with the pictures.

3. Build one or more of the six simple machines. You may want to use building toys and other old materials from home.

4. Write a report about an inventor and the invention.

5. Invent a special machine. Write a story or draw a picture of it. What can people do with the machine?

6. Make a safety poster on how to use machines safely.

Reading for Fun

A Book About Springs by Harlan Wade, Raintree Publishing, Ltd.: Milwaukee, © 1977.

Springs turn rods and wheels and still keep their shape.

Along Came the Model T! How Henry Ford Put the World on Wheels by Robert Quackenbush, Parents' Magazine Press: New York, © 1978.

Learn about the Model T car and then make your own.

Earth Movers by Mark Rich, Children's Press, Inc.: Chicago, © 1980.

Compare the size, strength, and speed of various large earth-moving machines.

Unit 3

Matter and Its Changes

Chapter One
What Is Matter?

How can we describe these objects? How could you describe an object to someone without giving its name?

Suppose your class is going to play kickball. You are sent to get the ball. In the gym, you find many kinds of balls. How will you choose the right one?

Describing Objects

People describe or tell about objects in many ways. Size and shape are used to describe objects. Color and texture also describe objects. Size, shape, color, and texture are all properties of objects. A **property** (PRAHP urt ee) is used to describe how an object looks, feels, or acts. What are some properties of the objects in these pictures? How can you use the properties to tell the cats apart?

Activity

How Can We Use Properties?

What to use:

students' shoes   pencil and paper

What to do:

1. Work with 5 other students. Put your shoes in one pile with the other students' shoes.

2. Have one student group the shoes into two piles based on one property.

3. Take turns guessing what property was used to group the shoes.

4. The first student who guesses correctly then groups the shoes based on a new property.

5. Record the properties used.

What did you learn?

1. How many properties were used?
2. What are some of the properties?

Using what you learned:

1. Describe the properties of one part of your clothes. See if a friend can tell what piece you are talking about.
2. How are the properties of dogs different from those of shoes? How are they alike?

Properties of All Objects

The objects shown here are all different. The objects are also alike in two ways. First, all objects take up space. Everything in this gym takes up space. What happens when two objects try to take up the same space?

Second, all objects have mass. **Mass** is how much there is of an object. You can measure the mass of an object. The unit used to measure mass is the **gram.** One gram is a small amount of mass. Two paper clips have a mass of about one gram. A nickel has a mass of about five grams.

Sometimes you may want to measure a large mass. Large amounts of mass are measured in kilograms (KIHL uh grams). A **kilogram** is 1000 grams. The mass of the boy is about 20 kilograms. What do you think your mass is?

Activity

How Much Mass?

What to use:

nickels   4 small objects   pencil and
paper clips   balance   paper

What to do:

1. Copy the chart. Predict the mass of each object.

2. Fill in the chart. Write what you predicted in order beginning with the most mass.

3. Put one object on the left side of the balance. Use the nickels and paper clips to balance the object.

4. Record the number of nickels and paper clips used.

5. Repeat steps 3 and 4 for the other objects.

What did you learn?

1. How well were you able to predict the mass of each object?

2. What object has the most mass?

Using what you learned:

1. How can you find out what the mass for each object is in grams? Try it and fill in the rest of the chart.

2. When would it be hard to find the mass of objects by using nickels and paper clips?

Looking at Matter

All objects that take up space and have mass are called **matter.** Rocks, clocks, bees, and trees are matter. Everything around you is made of matter. You are made of matter, too. How can you tell that you are matter?

It is easy to see matter that is large. You may use a hand lens to see matter that is small. What small matter have you seen? What matter is too small to be seen?

From far away, the turtle looks like it is all one piece. When you get closer, you see it is made of tiny sand grains. How might you see each sand grain by itself?

Each sand grain in the turtle is made of even smaller parts. All matter is made of very small parts. These small parts of matter are called **atoms.** Most atoms are too small to be seen.

Matter is the same because it is made of atoms. Matter is also different. It is different because there are many kinds of atoms. The atoms join to form small particles of matter. Some particles are made of one kind of atom. Gold is made of one kind of atom. Some particles have more than one kind of atom. Salt is made of two different atoms. Particles of matter have different properties because the atoms can be joined in many ways.

How is the matter in these objects different? How is the matter the same?

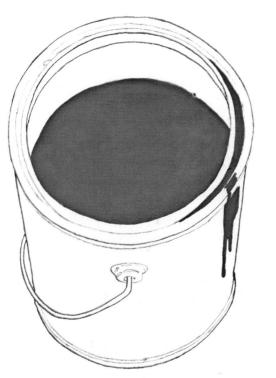

Chapter Review

Summary

- A property of an object describes how the object looks, feels, or acts.
- All objects take up space.
- All objects have mass.
- The mass of objects is measured in grams and kilograms.
- Matter is anything that takes up space and has mass.
- All matter is made of atoms.
- There are many kinds of atoms.

Science Words

property	kilogram
mass	matter
gram	atoms

Questions

1. List three of your favorite foods.
   (a) What are some properties of the foods?
   (b) Which of these properties are alike?
   (c) Which of these properties are different?
2. What are two properties that all matter has?
3. How many grams are in 3 kilograms?
4. What is an atom?
5. How are trees and rocks alike? How are they different?
6. Why are there so many kinds of matter?

Chapter Two
States of Matter

How many kinds of matter can you see here? Where might there be matter in the picture that you cannot see?

Properties describe matter. Wood, milk, and air have properties that put them in different groups. Wood, milk, and air are different states of matter. A **state** of matter is a group of matter with the same properties.

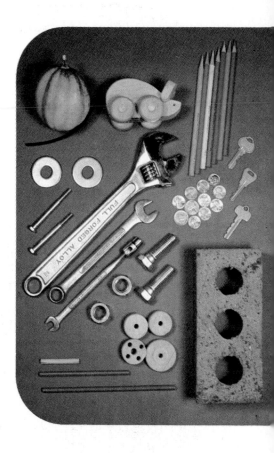

Matter in the Solid State

Wood is a solid. A **solid** has a certain size and shape. Most of the objects you see are in the solid state. Your desk is a solid. It does not change shape. Your desk also does not change size.

You can change the shape of some solids. How might you change the shape of a piece of chalk? How is the boy changing the shape of this solid? How can you change the shape of other solids?

Activity

How Much Space?

What to use:

jar	2 rubber bands	string
water	clay ball	paper towels

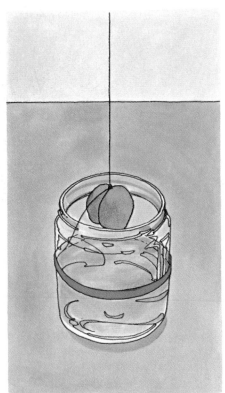

What to do:

1. Fill the jar half full of water. Mark the water level with one rubber band.

2. Tie the string around the clay. Lower the clay into the water.

3. Mark the new water level with the other rubber band.

4. Carefully lift the clay out of the water. Observe the water level.

5. Change the shape of the clay. Put it in the water. Observe the water level.

What did you learn?

1. What happened to the water level when you put the clay into the water?

2. What happened to the water level after you changed the shape of the clay? Why?

Using what you learned:

1. If you broke the clay into two pieces, how much space would they take up?

2. Tell why 10 grams of chopped nuts is the same amount as 10 grams of whole nuts.

Matter in the Liquid State

Milk is a liquid. A **liquid** is matter that has a certain size, or volume, but does not have a shape of its own. A liquid takes the shape of its container. What shape does juice in a pitcher have? What shape is the same juice in a glass? What happens to its shape when the juice spills?

Liquids flow. They can be poured. You can pour milk from a carton into a glass. Where else have you seen a liquid flow?

Liquids have a certain size. When you pour a certain amount of milk, its shape changes. The milk still takes up the same amount of space. It's size does not change.

Solid or Liquid?

What happens if you poke your finger into peanut butter? How is it like both a solid and a liquid? Some matter has properties of both states. What other objects are like both solids and liquids?

Activity

Is It a Solid or a Liquid?

What to use:

newspaper   mystery matter
small paper cup   paper towels

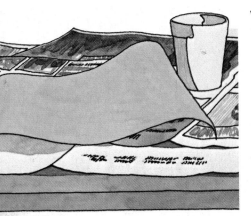

What to do:

1. Cover your desk with newspapers.

2. Get a cup of "mystery matter" from your teacher.

3. Carefully test the "mystery matter." Here are some things you might do.

   (a) Try to pour it.

   (b) Poke it with your fingers.

   (c) Roll it into a ball and try to bounce it on the desk.

What did you learn?

1. How was the "mystery matter" like a solid?

2. How was it like a liquid?

Using what you learned:

1. What other objects act like a solid and a liquid? List them.

2. How is each object on the list like a solid? How is each like a liquid?

Matter in the Gas State

Oxygen is a gas. A **gas** is matter that has no shape or size of its own. Oxygen takes the shape of any container it is in. Oxygen also spreads out to fill any size container. What happens if oxygen is moved from a large to a small container?

Oxygen and some other gases cannot be seen. They have no color. Air is many gases mixed together. You cannot see air. You can feel air when it moves. The wind is moving air.

Some gases have no odor. Air does not have an odor of its own. You may smell particles of matter that have mixed with air. What matter mixes with air and makes it smell good?

Activity

How Can You Pour Air?

What to use:

large bucket   2 clear cups   marking pen
water   masking tape

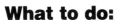

What to do:

1. Fill the bucket two-thirds full of water.

2. Label one cup A and one cup B.

3. Hold cup A right side up and push it under the water. Turn the cup upside down and hold it in the water.

4. Hold cup B upside down. Push it under the water.

5. Keeping both cups under the water, put cup B below cup A. Slowly turn cup B right side up. Observe what happens.

What did you learn?

1. What was in both cups when you first pushed them into the water?
2. What was in cup B after you turned it right side up?
3. What was in cup A when you finished?

Using what you learned:

1. How do you know that air takes up space?
2. What happened to the water in cup A?

Why Are States of Matter Different?

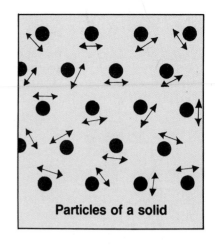

Particles of a solid

Atoms form particles of matter. These particles are moving. The particles in solids are shaking back and forth. In most solids, the shaking particles are packed close to each other. They form a definite pattern. Because of the pattern, solids do not change shape.

The particles in most liquids move faster than in solids. They are also farther apart. Particles in liquids fall over each other. They do not form a definite pattern. Liquids pour and change shape because of the way their particles move.

Gas particles move very fast. They are also very far apart from each other. They can spread out to fill any container. The same amount of gas can fill a small jar or a large room.

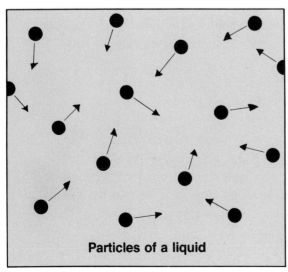

Particles of a liquid

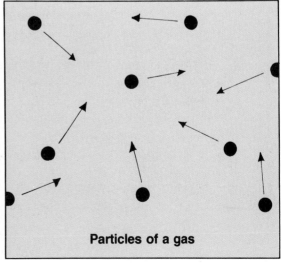

Particles of a gas

Tires from a Tree

What bounces and comes from trees? Rubber does. Rubber trees grow in hot, wet places. Many rubber trees grow in South America and Asia.

Some of the rubber you use starts as a liquid called latex. Workers called tappers cut a groove in the tree bark. The latex slowly drips out of the groove. It is caught in a cup. The latex looks like milk as it drips out.

The latex is then changed into rubber. First, it is heated and dried.

Then it is put in a machine that "chews" the rubber. The machine makes the rubber soft. The soft rubber can be made into tires, toys, and clothes.

Most of the rubber you use does not come from trees. It comes from chemicals. People can now make rubber from oil and coal. Why do you think most of the rubber is now made from chemicals? What do you use at home and at school that is made from rubber?

Chapter Review

Summary

- A state of matter is a group of matter with the same properties.
- Solid matter has a certain size and shape.
- Liquid matter has a certain size but not a certain shape.
- Some matter has the properties of solids and liquids.
- Gas matter has no size or shape of its own.
- Particles of matter in most solids are close together in a definite pattern.
- Particles of matter in most liquids are farther apart than in solids and do not have a definite pattern.
- Particles of matter in gases move very fast and are very far apart.

Science Words

state	**liquid**
solid	**gas**

Questions

1. Name a solid, a liquid, and a gas.
2. How are solids, liquids, and gases alike? How are they different?
3. You cannot see most gases. How do you know there are gases?
4. Why do liquids pour?
5. What state of matter is a pencil?
6. How can you change the shape of a nail and an orange?

Chapter Three

Changing States

How is matter changing here? What is causing the changes?

$\mathbf{Y}$ou are making juice for breakfast. You open the can but the juice does not pour out. After leaving the can on the counter for a while, you try to pour the juice again. This time, the juice pours out easily. What happened? Why could you pour the juice the second time you tried?

Solid to Liquid

Solid matter can change state. Solids **melt** when they change to the liquid state. You may have seen ice change to liquid water. Other solids melt, too. What solids have you seen melt?

Activity

How Can You Win the Race?

What to use:

ice cube   stopwatch
various materials   pencil and paper

What to do:

1. Think of ways to melt an ice cube.

2. Choose the way that you think will melt the ice cube in the shortest time.

3. Wait for your teacher's starting signal. Try the way you chose.

4. Record how long it takes for your ice cube to melt.

What did you learn?

1. What was the shortest time to melt an ice cube?

2. What way was used to melt the ice cube in the shortest time?

Using what you learned:

1. What could you do to keep an ice cube solid the longest time? Try it and record the results.

2. Why do some people put cold food in foam ice chests when they go on picnics?

Solids melt when they are heated. You know that particles of solids form a definite pattern. Heat makes the particles shake faster. Heat also makes the particles move apart. They no longer form a definite pattern. As the pattern breaks down, the solids change to liquids.

All solids do not melt at the same temperature. The frozen juice you made melted when it was put in a warm room. Where did the heat come from to melt the juice? Name another solid that melts in a warm room.

Most metals melt at much higher temperatures. Gold and silver may be melted to make jewelry. Melted steel can be made into beams and used for buildings. How else are metals used?

Liquid to Solid

Solids change to liquids when they melt. Liquids can also change state. Liquids **freeze** when they change to the solid state.

Liquids freeze when heat is removed from them. As heat is lost, the particles of matter move slower. They move closer together. The particles form a definite pattern. The liquid becomes a solid when the pattern forms.

What frozen liquids are in the pictures? What other frozen liquids have you seen? What caused these liquids to lose heat and freeze?

Activity

What Will Happen to the Water?

What to use:

shallow baking dish   tape
water   plastic wrap

What to do:

1. Place the dish by a window.

2. Fill the dish half full of warm water.

3. Tightly cover the top of the dish with plastic wrap.

4. Tape the plastic wrap to the dish.

5. Observe the dish each day for 2 days.

What did you learn?

1. What happened in the dish?
2. What caused the changes?

Using what you learned:

1. What do you think would happen if you took off the plastic wrap? Try it and find out.

2. How does this activity explain why bathroom mirrors sometimes become foggy?

Liquid to Gas and Gas to Liquid

Liquids can freeze. Liquids also can change to gases. You know that particles of liquids move. They bump into each other. Particles on top of a liquid may be bumped away from the rest of the liquid. The particles become a gas. The change from a liquid to a gas is **evaporation** (ih vap uh RAY shun).

Liquids evaporate at any temperature. Heat makes them evaporate faster. Why do you think heat speeds up evaporation?

Sometimes a gas may lose heat. As the gas cools, its particles move closer together. The gas will change to a liquid. The change from a gas to a liquid is called **condensation** (kahn den SAY shun). Where have you seen condensation?

Matter changes state when heat is added or taken away. What do you think would happen if the temperature of matter never changed? How would your life change if matter never changed state?

Chapter Review

Summary

- Solids melt when they change to liquids.
- Adding heat causes particles of matter to move faster and farther apart.
- Liquids freeze when they change to solids.
- Losing heat causes particles of matter to move slower and closer together.
- The change from a liquid to a gas is evaporation.
- The change from a gas to a liquid is condensation.
- Gaining or losing heat causes matter to change state.

Science Words

melt   **evaporation**
freeze   **condensation**

Questions

1. Where might you see each change of state in your home? When does each happen?
   - (a) melting
   - (b) freezing
   - (c) evaporation
   - (d) condensation
2. Why does water not form on the outside of a cup when you have a hot drink?
3. You are cooking stew. There is too much liquid in the pan. Why do you take the cover off the pan?
4. Water is added to the city swimming pool every day. Not all of the lost water was splashed out. What happens to some of the water?
5. What happens to the particles of matter when a liquid freezes?
6. Where does heat come from to melt ice in a glass?

Chapter Four
Changes and More Changes

What happened to these objects? How have they changed? Where have you seen matter change like this?

M atter is described by its properties. Sometimes properties of matter change. We can change the way matter looks. How are the girls changing matter? When have you changed matter the same way?

We Change Matter

The texture of matter can change. The wooden car felt rough at one time. The girl made it feel smooth. What made the texture of the wood change?

Some matter can be broken or bent. Some matter can be stretched or torn. Matter that is broken, bent, stretched, or torn changes shape. The matter may also change size. Name some matter you can change in shape or size. How can you change it?

Activity

Why Does the Dime Move?

What to use:

large empty soft drink bottle
freezer   eyedropper
water   dime

What to do:

1. Place the bottle in the freezer for ten minutes.

2. Put the cold bottle on a table. With an eyedropper, place a few drops of water on the rim of the bottle.

3. Cover the mouth of the bottle with a dime.

4. Observe the dime and the bottle for a few minutes.

What did you learn?

1. What happened to the dime?
2. What happened to the air in the bottle?

Using what you learned:

1. Why did the dime act as it did?

2. Why do you run hot water over a metal lid that is stuck on a glass jar?

Heat Changes Matter

Heat causes matter to change state. Heat causes matter to change in another way, too. Think of how a thermometer works. When the air warms, the liquid in the glass tube rises. The liquid rises because most matter expands (ihk SPANDZ) when it is heated. Matter that **expands** gets bigger and takes up more space. Most matter also contracts (kun TRAKTS) when it cools. Matter that **contracts** gets smaller and takes up less space. When will the liquid in the thermometer contract?

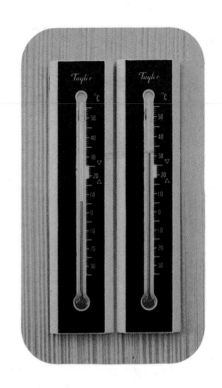

Matter that expands may cause problems. Tires get hot when you drive fast for a long time. What do you think happens to the air in the tires? What might happen if too much air is in a worn out tire?

Where have you seen matter expand? Where have you seen matter contract? How can this property of matter cause problems?

Making New Matter

Suppose you are going to make a cake. You mix the cake batter and pour it into a pan. Then you bake the cake. Compare the properties of the batter and the baked cake.

Sometimes one type of matter can be changed into another type of matter. Iron rusts. Rust forms when iron joins with oxygen. The properties of rust are different from those of iron or oxygen.

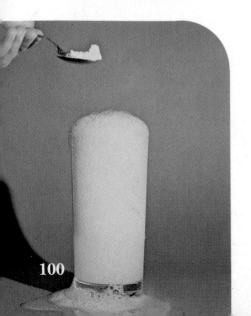

Burning causes new matter to form. When wood burns, it joins with oxygen in the air. What new matter is made when wood burns?

Mixing two kinds of matter together may make new matter. Some solids fizz when they mix with liquids. They make gas bubbles when they fizz. What have you mixed that bubbled and fizzed?

People and Science

A Special Artist

Who can play with clay all day? A potter can. Potters use clay to make pots, bricks, and tiles. Pots may be used to store food or carry water. Bricks and tiles are used to build homes.

Rosa is a potter. She likes to make pots. She starts by squeezing the clay in her hands. Squeezing the clay gets rid of air bubbles that may be in it. She then uses a potter's wheel to shape the clay. The wheel and clay spin. Rosa uses her hands to make different clay shapes.

Rosa likes to glaze her pots. This means that she paints the pots. She uses special paints to glaze her pots.

After the pots are glazed, Rosa fires them. Fire means to bake. Rosa puts the pots in a very hot oven called a kiln. Firing the clay makes some of the paints change color. Firing also makes the clay hard like glass. Why do you think potters fire their pots?

Time and Changes

Some changes in matter happen quickly. Glass breaking is a quick change. Some changes take a long time. What changes can you think of which take a long time?

The pictures show how one place changed in nine years. Which matter might have changed quickly? Which matter changed slowly?

Changes in matter can be helpful or harmful. Plants grown for food are a helpful change. Changing clay into building bricks is helpful, too. Name other helpful changes in matter. Rusting metal can be harmful. Garbage that is thrown into rivers can be harmful, too. How can burning wood be both helpful and harmful?

Chapter Review

Summary

- Properties of matter can be changed.
- Most matter expands when it is heated.
- Most matter contracts when it is cooled.
- One type of matter can be changed into another type of matter.
- Changes in matter may happen quickly or slowly.
- Changes in matter may be helpful, harmful, or both.

Science Words

expands   **contracts**

Questions

1. Name two ways that heat energy changes matter.
2. Why do people run hot water on jar lids that are too tight to open?
3. List two ways that each of the following types of matter can change.
   - (a) water
   - (b) milk
   - (c) puppy
   - (d) tree
   - (e) car
   - (f) paper
4. Name two helpful changes in matter.
5. Name two harmful changes in matter.
6. How can a bike change? Will the changes be fast or slow?
7. What makes most matter expand?
8. How are the properties of a loaf of baked bread different from the batter?

Self Checks

Answer these Self Checks on a sheet of paper.

1. In which of the following changes is new matter being made?

   (a) sawing wood   (d) fizzing tablets

   (b) rusting bike   (e) washing hands

   (c) freezing food   (f) burning logs

2. List two properties for each state of matter.

3. What makes up all matter?

4. What happens to the particles of matter when a liquid changes to a gas?

5. In what state of matter are the particles farthest apart?

6. What change of state is happening in each picture?

a

b

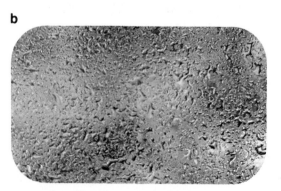

d

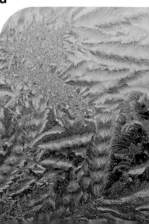

c

Idea Corner

More Fun with Science

1. Make a bulletin board display on changes of matter. Use magazine pictures or your own drawings.
2. Write a story telling how it would feel to be made of snow. What changes would happen to you?
3. Find three objects that have changed in your house. Draw how these objects have changed.
4. What helpful changes in matter can you make around your school?

Reading for Fun

The Inside Story of Metal by Norman F. Smith, Julian Messner: New York, © 1977.

Find out all about metals.

Small Worlds Close Up by Lisa Grillone and Joseph Gennaro, Crown Publishers Inc.: New York, © 1978.

Take a look at what matter looks like when viewed through an electron microscope.

Solids, Liquids, and Gases by Jeanne Bendick, Franklin Watts, Inc.: New York, © 1974.

What do solids, liquids, and gases have to do with matter?

Unit 4

Water Around Us

Chapter One

States of Water

Where do you see water here? What states of water are in the picture?

Water can be found in many places on Earth. Most water found on Earth is in the liquid state. Rivers and lakes have liquid water. Liquid water can even be found in the soil. Where else can liquid water be found?

Liquid Water

Pure liquid water is not found in many places. Most water has some dirt, salt, pieces of rock, or other objects in it. Pure water does not have any of these things. Pure water has no taste or odor.

Which water shown here would taste most like the water in your house? Why? How do you think each might smell? Where might you go to find water as shown in the pictures?

Activity

When Do the Liquids Freeze?

What to use:

3 plastic cups
masking tape
marking pen

liquids A, B, and C
3 thermometers
pencil and paper

What to do:

1. Label the cups A, B, and C. Fill cup A one-third full of liquid A. Fill cups B and C one-third full of liquids B and C.

2. Record the temperatures of each liquid.

3. Put the cups with the thermometers in a freezer. Record the temperatures every 15 minutes until all three are frozen.

4. Make a graph showing what happens to the temperature of each liquid.

What did you learn?

1. How did the temperatures change?
2. At what temperature did each liquid freeze?

Using what you learned:

1. Liquid A is water, B is water and vinegar, C is salt water. How does vinegar and salt affect the freezing temperature of water?

2. Antifreeze acts the same as salt in water. Why is it added to a car radiator in winter?

Water as a Solid

Water in the solid state can be found in many places. Ice, snow, and frost are water in the solid state. How is water as a solid different from water as a liquid? Liquid water can freeze. Pure water will freeze at 0° Celsius (SEL see us). **Celsius** is a scale people use to measure temperature. Each mark on the scale shows a change of one degree. Find the freezing temperature of pure water on the scale. What do you think °C means?

Winter is very cold in some places. The outside temperature often reaches 0°C. The temperature may even go below the 0°C point. You know that pure water freezes at 0°C. What do you think happens when the temperature goes above 0°C?

A **glacier** (GLAY shur) is a large river of ice. The ice forms from packed snow that falls for many, many years. The snow gets very deep. New snow pushes down on the old snow and changes it to ice. The ice then begins to move slowly. One glacier may move a long way. It may cover much land. Where might you find a glacier? Why are there no glaciers in Florida?

Some glaciers flow into the sea. Ice breaks off and floats away. Large blocks of floating glacier ice are called **icebergs.** Icebergs slowly melt as they float in the ocean. Ocean water is salty. What type of water forms icebergs?

People in ships must be very careful around icebergs. They know that most of an iceberg is below water. Why is it dangerous for a ship to sail too close to an iceberg?

Activity

How Do You Know There Is Water in the Air?

What to use:

paper towel

What to do:

1. Use a paper towel to dry the palm of one hand. Feel your palm.

2. Hold your palm 1 centimeter in front of your mouth.

3. Breathe deeply. Blow your breath onto your palm 8 times. Feel your palm again.

4. Wait one minute. Feel your palm again.

What did you learn?

1. Why did you wipe your palm with the paper towel in step 1?
2. How did your palm feel after blowing on it?
3. How did your palm feel after doing step 4?
4. How do you know water is in the air?

Using what you learned:

1. Try this activity using a window or mirror. Compare the results.
2. What happens to the windows inside a car on cool, rainy days? Why?

Water as a Gas

Water in the liquid state may change to water in the gas state. We say that the water evaporates. Water as a gas is called **water vapor.** Water vapor is one gas in the air. You cannot see water vapor. How can you tell when water evaporates?

Water evaporates from soil, rivers, lakes, and oceans. Animals breathe water vapor into the air. Plants release water vapor into the air, too.

The amount of water vapor in the air may change. Heat speeds up evaporation. Places that are hot and wet have more water vapor in the air. What places would have little water vapor in the air? Why?

◼◼◼Chapter Review

Summary

- Most of the Earth's water is found in the liquid state.
- Most water on Earth is not pure.
- Pure water freezes when it is 0° Celsius.
- Ice, snow, frost, glaciers, and icebergs are water in the solid state.
- Water vapor is a gas in the air.

Science Words

Celsius
glacier
icebergs
water vapor

Questions

1. What are the three states of water?
2. Where is water found in the liquid state?
3. Name some examples of water in the solid state.
4. At what temperature does water freeze?
5. Name a place where there is much water vapor in the air.
6. Tell how the properties of solid water are different from the properties of liquid water.
7. What does °C mean?
8. Tell how a glacier forms.

Chapter Two
Water in the Air

In what state is the water in the footprints? What is happening to the footprints? Where is the water going?

The water on the girl is a liquid. It changes to the gas called water vapor as she dries. What is the change from a liquid to a gas called?

Speeds of Evaporation

Water does not always evaporate at the same speed. Heat may make water evaporate faster. Wet clothes usually dry faster on warm, sunny days. How fast would the clothes dry on cool, cloudy days? Look at the footprints again. What kind of day do you think it is?

All air has some water vapor. Moist air has a lot of water vapor. Dry air has little water vapor. Dry air can take up more water vapor than moist air. Water evaporates faster in dry air.

Both of the places on the right are hot. Which place is hot and dry? Where would water evaporate faster?

Activity

How Can You Speed Up Evaporation?

What to use:

water   paper cup
2 washcloths   clock or watch

What to do:

1. Pour a cup of water on each washcloth.

2. Fold one washcloth in half. Fold it in half again.

3. Let the second washcloth lie flat.

4. Put both washcloths in a warm, dry place.

5. Observe how long it takes for each washcloth to dry.

What did you learn?

1. Which washcloth dried faster?
2. Why did it dry faster?

Using what you learned:

1. How could waving the washcloth change evaporation?
2. How would you hang clothes so they dry quickly?
3. What could you do to slow down evaporation? When would this be helpful?

Water evaporates only where it meets the air. Suppose you are at a lake. The lake is six meters deep. Which is evaporating, the water near the bottom or the water at the surface? Tell why.

Look at the two pans of water. In which pan does more water meet the air? The water will evaporate faster in one pan. Tell why. How can you check your answer?

Moving air speeds up evaporation too. Wet hair and clothes dry faster on windy days. Warm, dry, windy days are even better for drying clothes. How is a hair dryer like a warm, dry, windy day?

Activity

How Can Water Change from Gas to Liquid?

What to use:

2 shiny metal cans   water
ice cubes to fill one can   paper towels
food coloring

What to do:

1. Fill one can with ice cubes. Add a few drops of food coloring to the water. Fill the spaces around the ice cubes with the colored water.

2. Fill the second can with colored water.

3. Breathe on both cans. Observe what happens.

4. Wipe the outside of both cans with the paper towels.

5. Let the cans stand for 10 minutes. Observe what happens.

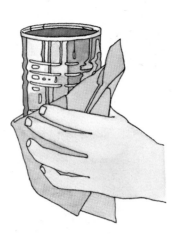

What did you learn?

1. What changes did you observe when you breathed onto the cans?

2. What caused the changes?

3. What happened to the cans after 10 minutes?

4. How was this change like the first change? How was it different?

Using what you learned:

1. Why was food coloring added to each can of water?

2. Make a list of places where you have seen this change take place before.

3. Why can you see your breath when you go outside on a cold day?

Condensation

Water vapor may condense to liquid water when it cools. The change is called condensation. **Dew** is a form of condensation. Dew may form on objects when the air cools at night. You can see the dew on cars and grass in the morning. Frost may form when the air is colder than 0°C. **Frost** is ice crystals that form on objects. What happens to dew and frost later in the day when the air warms?

Clouds

Clouds also form when water vapor condenses. The water condenses on very small pieces of matter, like dust, in the air. In cold air, the water vapor changes to small ice crystals. **Clouds** are made from millions of these drops or crystals. Clouds get bigger as more waterdrops or ice crystals form.

A cloud very close to the ground is called **fog.** Why does fog form when the air becomes cooler? What happens to fog when the air gets warmer?

Precipitation

Both the waterdrops or ice crystals in clouds are very small. They are so small they hang in the air. Sometimes the drops or crystals grow too large. When they grow large enough, they are too heavy to stay in the air. The drops or crystals fall to the ground. Water that falls from clouds is called **precipitation** (prih sihp uh TAY shun).

Rain and snow are two kinds of precipitation. Rain is liquid water that falls when the air is warmer than 0°C. Snow is made of ice crystals that fall when the air is colder.

Sleet and hail are two other kinds of precipitation. Sleet is frozen rain. Some hail is formed from many layers of ice. The picture shows hailstones. Why might it be dangerous to be out in a hailstorm?

123

A High-Flying Job

What can a farmer do when it does not rain? The answer is to hire a rainmaker.

Crops need rain to grow. Sometimes rain does not fall for many months. The crops die. That is when Grace goes to work. Grace is a rainmaker.

Rainmakers use different ways to make rain. Grace uses a small plane and dry ice. She flies her plane over a group of clouds. Then, she drops small pieces of dry ice into the clouds. This is called seeding the clouds. Water vapor in the air is cooled by the dry ice. The water vapor changes to snow. As the snow falls, it changes to rain. Rain does not always fall after Grace seeds the clouds. Sometimes enough water vapor is not in the air.

Grace likes her job. She knows the crops need rain to grow. Grace knows she is helping the farmer. Whom else does Grace help?

Chapter Review

Summary

- Liquid water evaporates into the air.
- Evaporation is faster in warm, dry air than in cool, moist air.
- Water evaporates at its surface.
- Wind speeds up evaporation.
- Condensation happens when water vapor cools.
- Dew, frost, clouds, and fog are forms of condensation.
- Clouds are made of small waterdrops or very small ice crystals.
- Precipitation is water that falls from the clouds.
- Rain, snow, sleet, and hail are forms of precipitation.

Science Words

dew   fog
frost   precipitation
clouds

Questions

1. How can evaporation be speeded up?
2. Why do people use clothes dryers to dry their clothes?
3. List two kinds of condensation.
4. What kind of precipitation falls when the air is warm?
5. Why does snow usually fall in winter?
6. Tell how clouds form.

Chapter Three
The Endless Cycle

What is happening? From where is the water coming? Where is the water going?

How much water do you use each day? You use water when you take a drink or wash your hands. You use water when you brush your teeth or water the lawn. Most people use water without knowing where it comes from. They do not know where the water goes. Most people never think about how important water is to their lives. How would your life change if the water in your home were turned off for one day?

Runoff

Precipitation brings water from the air back to the ground. Water from rain or melting snow may flow across the ground. Water that flows across the ground is called **runoff.**

Gravity makes runoff flow downhill. The water flows into small streams or ponds. The streams flow into rivers. The rivers become bigger as more streams flow into them. Finally, the rivers flow into oceans. Tell why large rivers are not found high in the mountains.

Runoff may cause some damage on land. Sometimes a very heavy rain causes rivers and streams to flow over their banks. A flood happens. Water from the flood flows quickly over the ground. Why would fast moving water cause damage? What would it damage?

Activity

Which Soaks Up More?

What to use:

2 different kinds of soil

2 large clear jars

masking tape

marking pen

small paper cup

water

stopwatch

pencil and paper

What to do:

1. Fill each jar half full with one of the soils. Pack down the soil with your hands.

2. Label each jar with the kind of soil.

3. Pour a cupful of water on the soil in each jar. Record how long it takes for the water to soak into the soil.

4. Add cupfuls of water to each jar until the soil cannot soak up any more. Record how many cupfuls each soil holds.

What did you learn?

1. Which soil soaks up water faster?
2. Which soil soaks up the most water?

Using what you learned:

1. Which soil would have the least amount of runoff during a heavy rain? Why?
2. Which kind of soil would have the biggest mud puddles after a heavy rain? Why?

Groundwater

Most runoff flows into streams, rivers, or oceans. However, some water soaks into the ground. The water moves into air spaces around pieces of soil. Water can even soak into rocks in the soil. Water that soaks into the ground is called **groundwater.**

Water under the ground does not stop moving. Some groundwater evaporates back into the air. Some groundwater is used by plants to make food. Some of the water is trapped between layers of rock. Gravity causes most groundwater to move downward. The water moves through soil and rocks. The water moves until it reaches places where it can flow onto the land again. Lakes, rivers, and swamps are places groundwater flows onto the land.

Water Storage

People in cities use large amounts of water. The water is stored in lakes or other places until it is used. A place that stores water is called a **reservoir** (REZ urv wor).

Ponds and rivers are reservoirs. A glacier is a reservoir, too. What is the largest reservoir you can think of? People build some reservoirs. Water towers are large tanks that store water. People build them on farms and in cities. Some tall buildings have water towers on their roofs. Why do you think water towers would be placed on a roof?

Soil stores water, too. Sometimes that water is deep in the ground. People dig wells to get the water. How can people use well water?

Activity

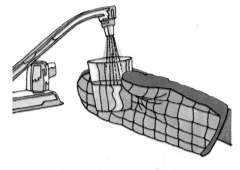

What Is the Water Cycle?

What to use:

clear tall plastic glass   plastic dish
oven mitt   4 to 5 ice cubes
hot water

What to do:

1. Hold the glass with the oven mitt. Fill the glass two-thirds full of hot water. Tilt the glass to wet the sides to the top.

2. Put some ice in a dish. Set the dish on top of the glass.

3. Observe what happens.

What did you learn?

1. What happened in the glass?
2. Where did evaporation take place?
3. Where did condensation take place?
4. Where did precipitation take place?

Using what you learned:

1. How does this activity show what happens to some lake water?
2. How does the activity show how clouds form?
3. How does the activity show a water cycle?

The Water Cycle

Water is moving. Water is changing states. Much of it is changing state right now. Water is evaporating from the soil, streams, lakes, and oceans. It is condensing to form clouds and precipitation. On the ground, water is being stored in reservoirs. Each change is part of a cycle. The cycle never ends. The evaporation, condensation, precipitation, and storage of water are all parts of the **water cycle.**

The water you drink now may have been snow last month. Next year the same water may be stored in a lake. All of the water on Earth has been changing in the water cycle. It moves and changes over and over. How can the water stored as snow become water in the ocean?

A Drop in the Cycle

How does it feel to be a drop of water in the ocean? It is mixed up and crowded. Deep in the water crowd it is dark and cold. Close your eyes tightly. Wrap your arms around yourself and squeeze hard. See the darkness! Feel the cold—burr-r! Feel the other drops squeezing you! They are pushing you upward!

Relax your arms. Relax your eyes. It is getting lighter! The sun is warming you! You are moving upward, faster and faster. It is exciting and you feel good. Pop! You have evaporated.

Sit taller and taller. You are rising in the air as water vapor. Now it is getting colder and colder. Curl into a ball. You are becoming smaller and smaller. Clunk! You have condensed! Wave your arms softly. You are a tiny drop in a cloud floating gently in the air. Ahh! It feels great. The view is beautiful as you are pushed over the land. There is a city. Bump! Swell up. You are getting bigger. Bump! You are getting still bigger. Other drops are bumping and holding onto you. Help! Help! You are falling! Curl up. You are precipitating. Faster and faster you fall. Splat! Flatten out. You have landed in a pond.

Make a circle with your head. You are spinning around, faster and faster. It is crowded. You are moving quickly through a dark pipe. Splash! Flatten out. Suddenly you are in a shower mixed with soap. Yuk! Make a bad face. The soap makes you feel very bad.

Make circles with your head. You are spinning again. Slurp! Curl up. It is crowded in the drainpipe. You do not feel so good. There is light ahead. Splash! Flatten out. You are dumped into a river. Why are the fish swimming away from you? You want to play. They swim away.

Now it is getting warmer. Pop! You have evaporated again. You feel good. The soap stayed in the river. Your world will always change. You are a drop in the water cycle. You will never leave the cycle! Sit calmly with your eyes closed. Think about the water cycle.

The picture below shows the changes of the water cycle. Tell about each change in the water cycle. Where is each change happening here? Why are all of these changes called a water cycle?

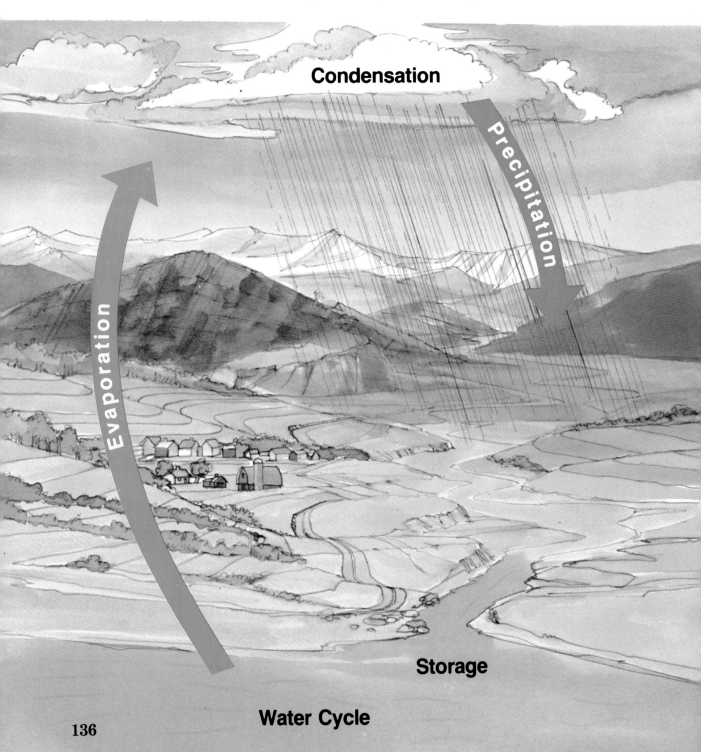

Condensation

Precipitation

Evaporation

Storage

Water Cycle

Chapter Review

Summary

- Water flowing over the ground is called runoff.
- Water that soaks into the ground is called groundwater.
- Gravity causes runoff and groundwater to flow downhill.
- Reservoirs are places where water is stored.
- Water is moving and changing state on the Earth.
- All the water on Earth is part of the water cycle.

Science Words

runoff
groundwater
reservoir
water cycle

Questions

1. How is water stored in the soil?
2. How do people get stored water out of the soil?
3. Where does runoff water go?
4. What reservoirs are near your home?
5. How is groundwater different from runoff?
6. How can a drop of water from the ocean fall as a snowflake in the hills?
7. List three ways you use water.
8. Explain the water cycle.

Unit 4 Review

✓ Self Checks

Answer these Self Checks on a piece of paper.

1. Which of these pictures show reservoirs made by people?
2. List ways people use the water stored in each reservoir above.
3. How can people help keep water clean during the water cycle?
4. How does temperature affect each change of state in the water cycle?
5. Place the letters of the pictures in order. Begin with the picture showing where evaporation happens the fastest.

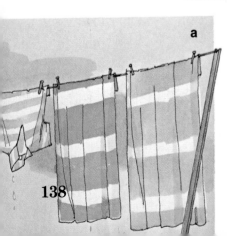

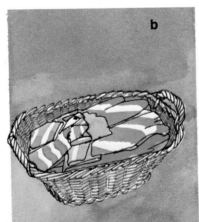

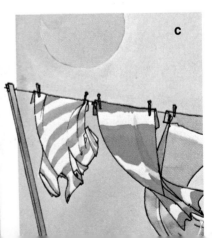

138

Idea Corner

More Fun with Science

1. Find a place to sit by yourself outside. Where is each change of the water cycle happening around you? Which changes can you see happening?
2. Make a bulletin board showing different kinds of precipitation.
3. Plan an activity to see what will speed up the rate of evaporation. You might want to try some of the following ideas:
   (a) amount of water   (c) temperature
   (b) amount of wind
4. Find out about a reservoir in your area. Is it natural or made by people? How is the water used in this reservoir?

Reading for Fun

Clean Air—Clean Water for Tomorrow's World by Reed Millard, Julian Messner: New York, © 1977.
    Problems and solutions to water pollution are discussed in this book.

Follow the River by Lydia Dabcovich, E. P. Dutton: New York, © 1980.
    Follow a river from its source to the sea.

Glaciers: Nature's Frozen Rivers by Hershell M. Nixon and Loan L. Nixon, Dodd, Mead, and Co.: New York, © 1980.
    Learn more about glaciers.

Unit 5

Chapter One

Living Things
Need Food

What are these animals doing? What do you think is going to happen?

All living things need food. Plants use food as they grow. Animals use food as they grow. People use food as they grow, too. Living things also use food to keep their bodies healthy. All living things use food for energy, too. Without food, plants, animals, and people would die.

How Much Food

Living things use different amounts of food. Many kinds of birds eat almost all day. This snake may not eat again for several days. Why do you think the snake eats less often than the bird? How much food do you think an elephant eats?

Plants Make Food

Green plants make their own food. Plants use sunlight, water, and air when they make food. You know that most of the food is made in the plant's leaves. What would happen to a rosebush if it lost all of its new leaves in the spring?

Plants make more food than they use. The food that is not used is stored in many plant parts. Some food is stored in roots. Turnips and carrots have large amounts of stored food. Food may be stored in stems. Sugar cane has a large amount of stored food in its stem. Some food is also stored in leaves. What leaves do you eat that have stored food?

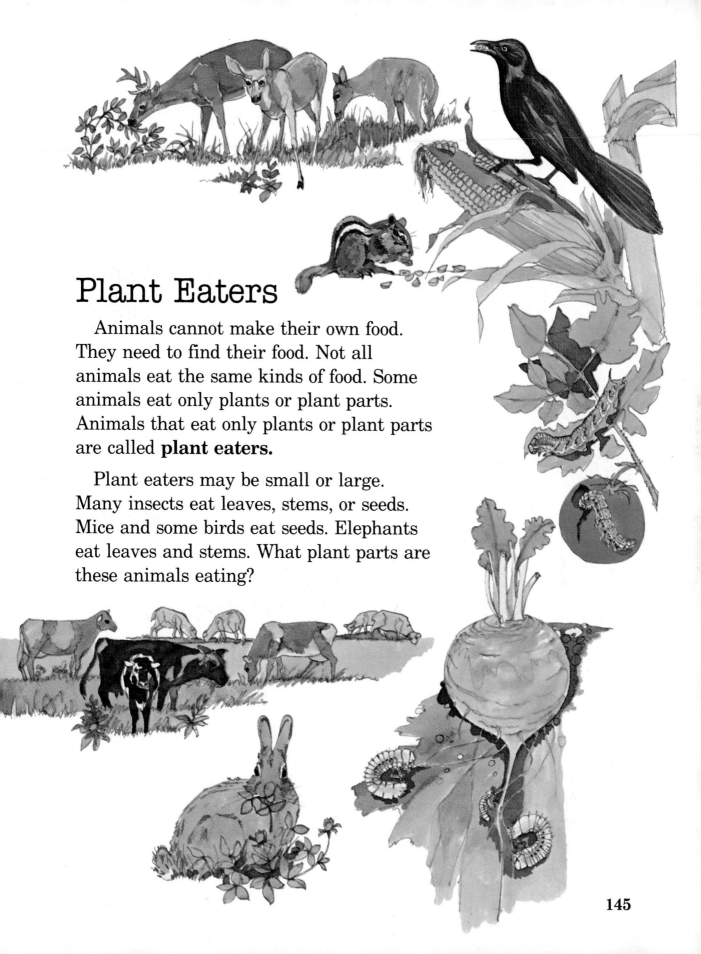

Plant Eaters

Animals cannot make their own food. They need to find their food. Not all animals eat the same kinds of food. Some animals eat only plants or plant parts. Animals that eat only plants or plant parts are called **plant eaters.**

Plant eaters may be small or large. Many insects eat leaves, stems, or seeds. Mice and some birds eat seeds. Elephants eat leaves and stems. What plant parts are these animals eating?

145

What Plant Part Is Eaten?

What to use:

small plant-eating animal   water
glass or wire cage   mixed seeds
animal bedding   lettuce
jar or dish   carrot

What to do:

1. Prepare a proper cage for the animal.

2. Place different plant parts in the cage.

3. Gently put the animal in the cage.

4. Observe what, when, and how the animal eats for two or three days.

5. Put fresh food and water in the cage each day. Clean the cage each day.

What did you learn?

1. What did the animal eat?
2. When and how did the animal eat?

Using what you learned:

1. Suppose your animal got out of its cage. How could you use what you learned in this activity to catch the animal?
2. Pandas eat only one kind of leaf. Would your animal or a panda be better able to find food? Why?

Animal Eaters

What is happening in the picture? Which animal is eating? What is being eaten?

Some animals eat only other animals. An animal that hunts and eats other animals is called a **predator** (PRED ut ur). Wolves, snakes, and cats are predators. They may eat squirrels, mice, or birds.

Predators are an important part of nature. Suppose foxes were the only animals that ate rabbits. What would happen to the number of rabbits if all the foxes died? How could killing all the foxes hurt the rabbits?

Animals eaten by predators are called **prey.** Which of these animals are prey? Which are the predators? How can an animal be both a predator and a prey?

148

Plant and Animal Eaters

Some animals eat both plants and animals. Bears may eat fish and nuts or berries. Raccoons eat meat. They also eat fruits and seeds. Suppose two animals live in the same area. One animal eats only plants. The other eats both plants and animals. Which animal might be able to find more food if rain did not fall for many months? Why?

Most people eat both plants and animals. Some people eat only plants or plant parts. People who eat only plants must choose foods wisely. People who eat meat must also choose foods wisely. Everyone needs to choose foods that are good for their health. What plants did you eat today? What animals did you eat?

149

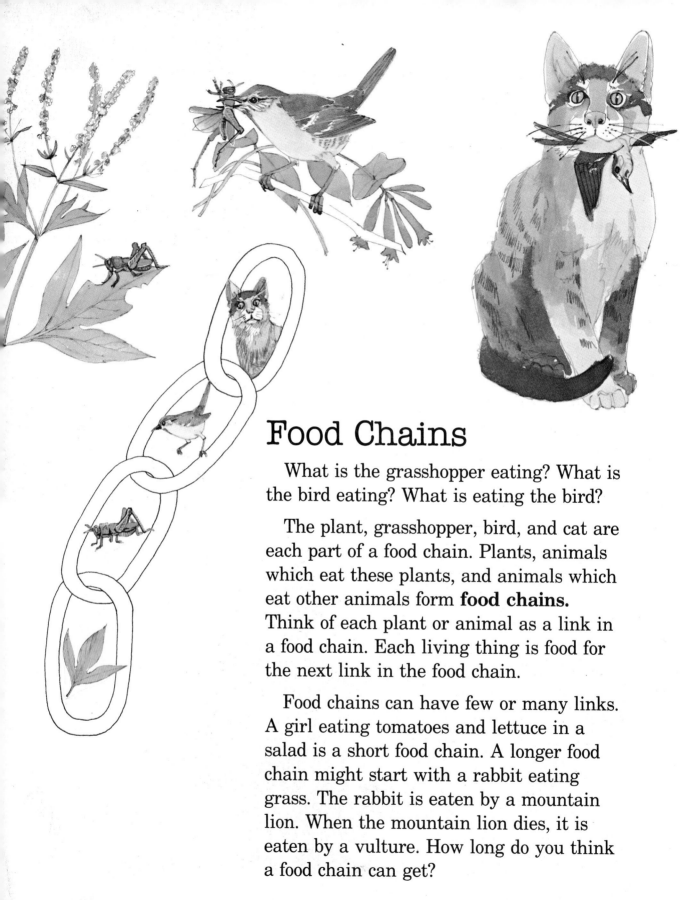

Food Chains

What is the grasshopper eating? What is the bird eating? What is eating the bird?

The plant, grasshopper, bird, and cat are each part of a food chain. Plants, animals which eat these plants, and animals which eat other animals form **food chains.** Think of each plant or animal as a link in a food chain. Each living thing is food for the next link in the food chain.

Food chains can have few or many links. A girl eating tomatoes and lettuce in a salad is a short food chain. A longer food chain might start with a rabbit eating grass. The rabbit is eaten by a mountain lion. When the mountain lion dies, it is eaten by a vulture. How long do you think a food chain can get?

All food chains begin with a producer (proh DEW sur). Any living thing which makes or produces its own food is called a **producer.** Plants are producers. They are the first link in a food chain.

The next link in all food chains is a consumer. A **consumer** is any living thing that must eat other living things for food. A consumer cannot make its own food. Every link that is added to a food chain after the first link is a consumer.

Suppose a shrimp eats some water plants. A small fish catches and eats the shrimp. A large salmon eats the small fish. Finally, a boy catches and eats the salmon. Which living thing in this food chain is a producer? Which living things in the chain are consumers?

Activity

How Many Food Chains Can You Make?

What to use:

small cards   paper punch
pencil   yarn

What to do:

1. Write the names of these plants and animals on the cards. Only one name should be on each card.

2. Punch a hole at the end of each card.

3. Make as many food chains as you can. Join each card or link with yarn.

4. Hang your food chains in class.

What did you learn?

1. How many links were on your longest food chain?

2. What was the first link of each chain?

3. Which animals were part of more than one food chain?

Using what you learned:

1. Tell why you cannot have two producers in any one of the food chains you made.

2. How can a plant or animal be part of more than one food chain?

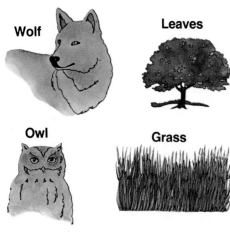

Wolf   Leaves

Owl   Grass

Corn

Mouse

Fish

Cow

Deer

Cat

Person

Grasshopper

Chapter Review

Summary

- All living things need food.
- Green plants make their own food.
- Some animals eat only plants.
- Predators eat other animals.
- Prey are animals eaten by predators.
- Some animals eat both plants and animals.
- Food chains are made of plants and animals.
- The first link in all food chains is a producer.
- Consumers cannot make their own food.

Science Words

plant eaters	**food chains**
predator	**producer**
prey	**consumer**

Questions

1. How can an animal be both predator and prey?
2. What living thing can make its own food? Where can the food be stored?
3. Name one animal that eats only plants, one that eats only animals, and one that eats both.
4. If a polar bear eats a seal, which animal is the predator? Which animal is the prey?
5. Why are plants the first link in a food chain?
6. How is a producer different from a consumer?

Chapter Two

Living Things and Their Needs

Where does this alligator live? Where do these plants live? Why do these living things live in the same place?

Your class goes to the zoo. While there you see lions, polar bears, lizards, and other land animals. The next day your class goes to the aquarium. You see sharks, squids, and seahorses. Each of the animals is in a different section of the zoo and aquarium. Each section looks like the place where the animals used to live. Why do you think each section looks different?

Plant and Animal Needs

Plants and animals live in almost every place on Earth. Not all living things can live in the same places. Each kind of living thing lives in the place where its needs are met. A **need** is any thing a plant or animal must have to stay alive. If a plant's needs are not met, it will die. If an animal's needs are not met, it will also die.

Food and Water

You know all living things need food.
Plants make their own food. They must
have water, air, and light to make their
own food. Not all plants need the same
amounts of water, air, and light. How
much light and water do the plants in the
pictures above need?

You know animals cannot make their
own food. Animals live in the same places
where the plants or animals they eat live.
Animals also live where they can find
water to drink. Some animals need large
amounts of water. Name some animals
that need a lot of water.

Shelter

Living things need shelter. A **shelter** is a place or object that protects plants or animals. Plants may need protection from wind, rain, and cold or hot temperatures. Some plants may start growing next to large rocks. The rocks may keep strong winds from blowing the young plants down. Sometimes plants grow close together in groups. Tall trees may be protection for other trees and plants from wind and too much light. What is protecting these plants? Why do they need to be protected?

Animals use shelters for protection from wind, rain, and temperatures, too. They also use shelters to hide from predators. Some animals may use caves for shelter. Others may use holes in trees and rocks. Some animals may dig burrows or tunnels under the ground. Prairie dogs and chipmunks dig burrows. What kind of shelter do many birds build? Where are some of these shelters built?

Some animals are protected from predators in other ways. They may live in large groups called herds, flocks, or packs. Most predators kill prey that are young, old, sick, or all alone. Usually they do not attack animals that are in a group. The group is like a shelter for each animal.

A group can also protect some animals from storms. During a storm, the animals move close to each other. Some animals are more protected than if they were alone.

What type of shelter do you have? How is your shelter like those of plants? How is it like those of other animals?

Space

You know that all living things need food, water, and shelter. All living things also need a certain amount of space. If too many plants or animals are in one place, their needs cannot be met.

Suppose you planted a garden. You put fifty seeds in a small area. All of the seeds sprouted. At first all of the seedlings grew well. The next week, some of the plants began to get yellow and wilt. Soon those plants died. The plants left did not look healthy. Too many plants were in one area. All of the plants could not get enough water and light.

The same thing would happen if too many rabbits lived in one place. All of the rabbits could not live. What may happen if too many people lived in one place?

Habitats

The place where each plant or animal lives is called a **habitat** (HAB uh tat). There are many kinds of habitats. A bird may have a nest in a tree. The nest and tree are part of its habitat. The habitat is also where the bird finds food and water.

A fish may live in a pond or a fishbowl. How are these two habitats different? How are they the same?

Activity

How Do You Make a Land Habitat?

What to use:

large widemouth jar	small plants
lid with small holes	water
metric ruler	water dish
gravel	small animal
potting soil	animal food
paper cup	pencil and paper
small rocks	

What to do:

1. Put a layer of gravel 3 cm deep in the jar. Put a layer of soil 8 cm deep on top of the gravel. Add a few small rocks on top of the soil.

2. Carefully place the plants in the soil. Add water until the soil is moist.

3. Measure how tall the plants are. Record their heights.

4. Fill the water dish and place it in the jar. Put some food next to the dish.

5. Put the small animal in the jar. Replace the lid.

6. Observe the habitat each day for two weeks. Add food and water for the animal each day.

What did you learn?

1. What was shelter for the plants in this activity?
2. What was the animal's shelter?
3. How do you know if the needs for the plants and animals were met?

Using what you learned:

1. How is this habitat the same or different from the animal's natural habitat?
2. What would happen if you planted these plants in an aquarium? Why?

Habitats may be small or large. Some habitats may be as small as a crack in a rock. Other habitats may be as large as a whole forest.

A habitat can be on land or in water. Fields, forests, and backyards are land habitats. What other land habitats can you name? Streams, puddles, ponds, and oceans are water habitats. Water habitats can be made of fresh water or salt water. Which picture shows an ocean habitat? How is it different from a lake habitat?

People Affect Habitats

The number of people on Earth keeps growing. There are billions more people now than a few hundred years ago. More people use more land. They use more water. People now live in places where only plants and animals used to live.

People change the natural habitats of living things. Some changes may be harmful to the plants and animals. There may be less food and water for them to use. There may be less space for the plants and animals. Some changes may be helpful. People might stop the erosion of some soil and rocks.

People need to be careful about changing habitats. They must conserve as many habitats as they can. **Conserve** means to use wisely. People conserve when they make wise decisions about how to use the land. How can people conserve the natural habitats of living things?

A Lion in the Trees

When does a lion live in a tree? A real lion lives on the ground. Golden lion marmosets live in the trees. Marmosets are monkeys. They have soft, golden manes like lions. Most of these monkeys are small. They are about the same size as squirrels. Many marmosets have tails that are longer than the rest of their bodies.

Marmosets do not eat the same food as real lions. They use their long, thin fingers to catch spiders and insects. They also eat fresh fruits. Marmosets live in hot, wet forests. They jump from tree to tree during the day. At night, they find holes in the trees. They sleep in these holes.

Marmosets are endangered. This means that there are not many living today. Some people are changing the monkeys' habitat. They are cutting down their tree homes. The small monkeys have few places to live. A few people try to capture the marmosets. They keep the monkeys for pets. Sometimes they sell the monkeys for pets to people in other countries.

Some people are trying to help the marmosets. The monkeys are taken to a safe place. This safe place is called a wildlife refuge. There are many trees for homes. There is much food to eat. The monkeys cannot be captured and sold for pets. Maybe the marmosets in the wildlife refuge will be saved. What else might people do to protect the marmosets?

Chapter Review

Summary

- Plants and animals live where their needs are met.
- All living things need food, water, shelter, and space.
- A habitat is any place where a plant or animal lives.
- All living things cannot live in the same kind of habitat.
- People can make helpful or harmful changes in habitats.

Science Words

need
shelter
habitat
conserve

Questions

1. Tell why a frog could or could not live in a place that was very dry.
2. How can flowers be protected from very cold, windy weather?
3. How is a young elephant protected by its herd?
4. Why do living things need space to live?
5. Tell two ways a land habitat is different from a water habitat.
6. List three living things. Tell what kind of habitat each plant or animal would live in.

Chapter Three

Living Things
and Their Habitats

What is wrong with this picture? What
should be done to make it right?

Plants and animals live in all parts of the world. They live on high mountains. They live in deep oceans. Living things are found in hot and cold places. They are found in dry and wet places. Why are some living things found in one place and not another? Why can a polar bear live in a cold place? Why would a polar bear die in a hot, dry place?

Living Things Are Adapted

Each living thing is adapted (uh DAP tud) to live in a certain place. **Adapted** means the living thing fits into its habitat. Its needs are met. The lizard and hippos are adapted to their habitats. How is the lizard adapted to where it lives? How are the hippos adapted to where they live?

Polar Habitats

Some parts of the world are very cold. These cold places near the North and South Poles are **polar areas.** Snow and ice cover the polar areas most of the year.

Few plants live in the polar areas. The plants can grow only in the short summer season. They cannot grow very large.

South Pole

Penguin

Seal

North Pole

Polar bear

Walrus

The same kinds of animals do not live in both polar areas. Polar bears and musk oxen live near the North Pole. Penguins live only near the South Pole. Find the North and South Poles on a map. Why do you think the same kinds of animals do not live in both places?

Some animals in these cold places look different in each season. Many grow heavy fur in winter. They shed much of their fur in summer. Some are adapted to season changes in other ways. How are the animals below adapted?

Musk ox

Arctic hare

Ptarmigan

Ermine

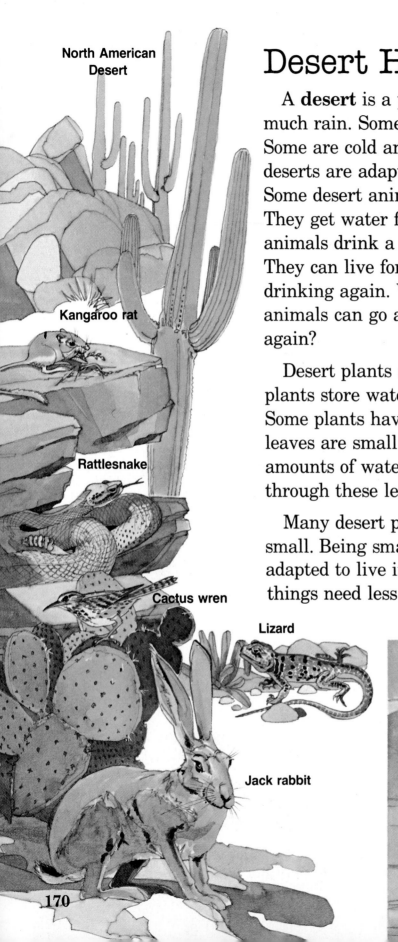

North American
Desert

Kangaroo rat

Rattlesnake

Cactus wren

Lizard

Jack rabbit

Desert Habitats

A **desert** is a place that does not have much rain. Some deserts are hot and dry. Some are cold and dry. Living things in deserts are adapted to having little water. Some desert animals drink little water. They get water from their food. Some animals drink a lot of water at one time. They can live for many days before drinking again. Which of these desert animals can go a long time before drinking again?

Desert plants are also adapted. Some plants store water in their stems or roots. Some plants have special leaves. The leaves are small and thin. Only small amounts of water move out of the plants through these leaves.

Many desert plants and animals are small. Being small is one way they are adapted to live in the desert. Small living things need less water than large ones.

Asian Desert

Camel

170

Grassland Habitats

A **grassland** is a place where most of the plants are grasses. Many different kinds of animals live on grasslands. Some of the biggest land animals live here. Some of the fastest live here, too. Where might you find the animals shown in each picture? How are they adapted to where they live?

Grasslands

171

Forest Habitats

There are different kinds of forest habitats. Some have four seasons each year. One forest habitat that has four seasons is the **temperate** (TEM prut) **forest.** A temperate forest has many trees that lose their leaves in fall. Maple trees lose their leaves in fall. What other trees would you find in a temperate forest?

Another kind of forest habitat has mostly evergreen trees. They do not lose their leaves in fall. Name some evergreen trees that you might find in a forest.

Forest animals are adapted to the change of seasons. For most of the year, they have a good supply of food. In winter, there is less food. The animals cannot find many leaves, fruits, nuts, and insects. The ground is cold and may be covered with snow. Some forest animals sleep through most of the winter.

Temperate Forest

Owl

Squirrel

Opossum

Black bear

Rabbit

Deer

Rain forests are very hot and wet habitats. Some rain forests are in South America and Africa.

Plants grow well in rain forests. They grow well because of the heat and rain. Many kinds of plants grow very close together. Tall trees grow above the bushes and vines.

Animals in rain forests are adapted to moving through the many plants. Monkeys have long tails and arms. They can swing from tree to tree. Tree frogs have feet that are like suction cups. They use their feet to move on the wet plants. Look at each animal. How is it adapted to move in a rain forest?

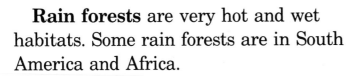

Rain Forest

Monkey

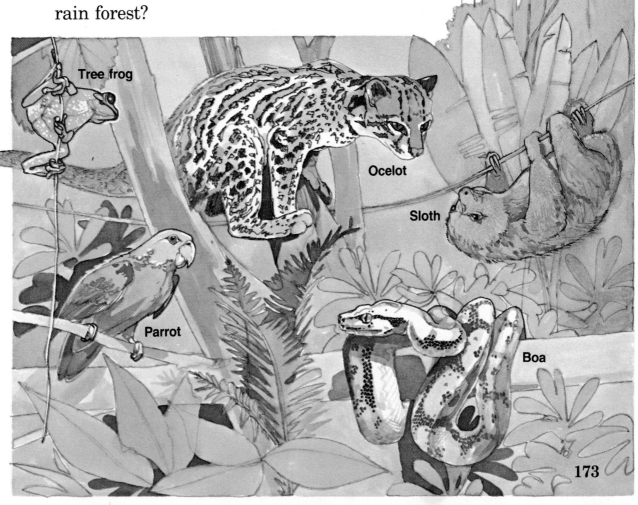

Tree frog

Ocelot

Sloth

Parrot

Boa

173

Water Habitats

Much of the Earth is covered with water. A water habitat is any place filled with water in which plants or animals live. Fresh water flows in lakes and rivers. Oceans are filled with salt water. Why are the living things in salt water different from those in fresh water?

Ocean Habitat

Shark

Anemone

Octopus

Starfish

174

Water animals need oxygen. A few water animals breathe with lungs. Most water animals have gills. Gills get oxygen from the water.

Many animals in the water move to find food and get away from predators. Other animals are attached to objects in the water. They get food as it floats past.

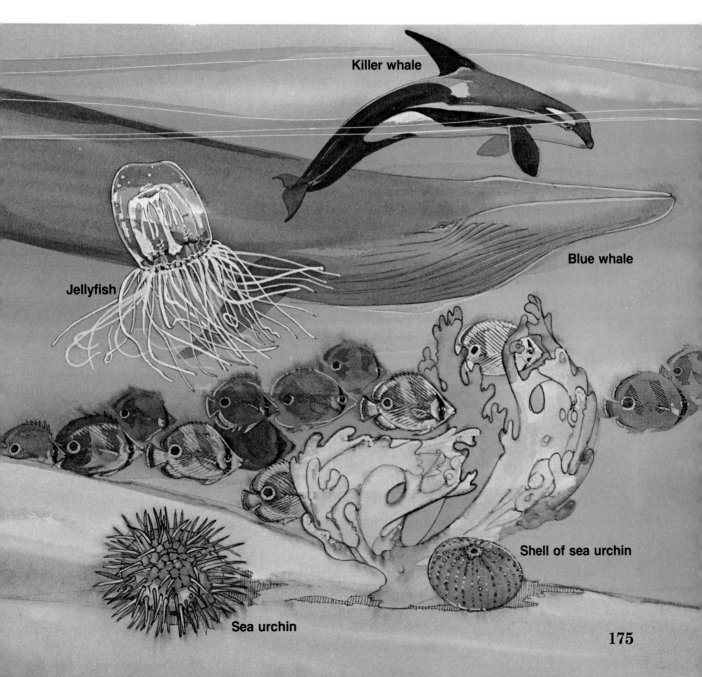

Killer whale

Blue whale

Jellyfish

Shell of sea urchin

Sea urchin

Activity

Where Do These Plants and Animals Live?

What to use:

crayons
drawing paper

What to do:

1. Look at these plants and animals. Decide where each one lives.

2. Choose one plant. On a sheet of paper, draw that plant in its habitat.

3. Choose two animals. On separate sheets of paper, draw the animals in their habitats.

What did you learn?

1. In which habitats do the animals live?
2. In which habitat does the plant live?
3. Which plants and animals live in the same kind of habitat?

Using what you learned:

1. How is the plant you drew adapted to its habitat?
2. How are the animals you drew adapted to their habitats?
3. Draw a picture of you in your habitat. How are you adapted to your habitat?

176

Where People Live

Most plants and animals live in only one kind of habitat. People are different. People can live in many kinds of habitats. People can change the food they eat. They can build the shelters they need. People can move from one place to another.

Each picture shows a different habitat where people live. What is each habitat like?

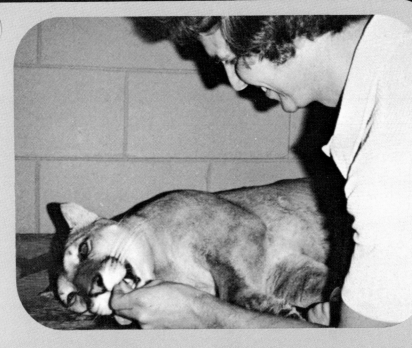

Treating a Giant Toothache

How do you treat a mountain lion or an elephant with a toothache? One zoo calls Dr. Schmitt. Dr. Schmitt is a dentist. He is a dentist for people. He is a dentist for animals, too.

People may think it is strange for a zoo to call a dentist. The zoo must make sure its animals stay healthy. If an animal gets sick, the zoo calls a veterinarian. If an animal gets a toothache, the zoo calls Dr. Schmitt.

Some zoo animals get toothaches from breaking their teeth. They break their teeth while chewing on cage bars. If the teeth are not fixed the animals might get sick.

Dr. Schmitt does not work on animals that are awake. He works on them when they are put to sleep. He must work fast to get done. He does not want his hand in the lion's mouth when it wakes up.

Most of the animals are too big for dentist tools. Dr. Schmitt uses some other tools instead. He uses a garden hose to wash out large mouths. He uses a vacuum cleaner to clean and dry the mouths. He also uses a large power drill to drill the teeth.

Dr. Schmitt helps the animals stay healthy. What other workers help animals that live in zoos?

Chapter Review

Summary

- Living things are adapted to their habitats.
- Polar areas are very cold most of the time.
- Deserts do not have much rain.
- Most of the plants on grasslands are grasses.
- Temperate forests have four seasons.
- Rain forests are always hot and wet.
- Water habitats are made of fresh or salt water.
- People can live in many habitats.

Science Words

adapted	grassland
polar areas	temperate forest
desert	rain forests

Questions

1. Why are all living things not able to live in the same kind of habitat?
2. In what habitat would a camel live? Why?
3. How is a whale adapted to its habitat?
4. Why can people live in most habitats?
5. List three habitats. Tell what kinds of plants live in each habitat.
6. Why can giraffes live in grasslands and not deserts?
7. How do some polar animals change with the seasons?
8. What do some animals do in the temperate forest during winter? Why?

Unit 5 Review

 Self Checks

Answer these Self Checks on a sheet of paper.

1. List three needs of all living things.

2. In what habitats do these plants and animals live?
   (a) fish   (c) alligator   (e) lion
   (b) cactus   (d) lizard   (f) tulip

3. Draw an animal that is adapted to a hot habitat. Tell how it is adapted.

4. What is a predator?

5. What is the difference between a producer and a consumer?

6. What kind of shelter would each of these living things need? Tell why each needs protection.
   (a) seedling in early spring   (c) person
   (b) young lamb   (d) bird

7. How can people protect a habitat?

8. Which is the better example of a food chain? Why?

Idea Corner
More Fun with Science

1. Make a drawing or collect pictures of animals that live in the (a) rain forest, (b) desert, (c) ocean, and (d) North and South Poles.
2. Make a map showing where different plants and animals live near you.
3. Draw two or three habitats for a beetle, a worm, or a cricket.
4. Choose a habitat. Invent an animal that is adapted to this habitat. Tell about or draw this animal.
5. Write a report about what people in your community are doing to conserve their habitat.
6. Exchange letters with a science class from another part of the country. Compare your habitats.

Reading for Fun

How Animals Hunt by J. M. Prince, Lodestar Books: New York, © 1980.
Find out how predators track and capture their prey.

Roadrunner by Naomi John, Unicorn Press: Greensboro, NC, © 1980.
How is the roadrunner both a predator and prey?

Seasons of the Tallgrass Prairie by Carol Lerner, William Morrow Co.: New York, © 1980.
How does the prairie change from season to season?

Unit 6

Rocks in Our World

Chapter One
How Are Rocks Formed?

What is the girl doing? Why did she choose this place? What other places might she go?

Kate and her grandfather take many long walks. Her grandfather points out interesting objects as they walk. On one walk he gave Kate a shiny stone. The stone had one color. He told Kate to look for another stone just like it. Kate could only find stones which had many colors. Only parts of her stones looked like the shiny stone. Why was it hard for Kate to find a stone of one color?

Minerals

The shiny stone was a mineral (MIHN uh rul). A **mineral** is a nonliving solid that is part of the Earth. Some minerals are shiny. Some have bright colors. Some may look clear like glass.

Certain minerals may be very hard. Others are very soft. How are these minerals being used? Which is hard? Which is soft?

185

Rocks

Rocks are made of minerals. Rocks of one mineral are one color. Rocks of many minerals may have many colors. Most rocks are made of many minerals. Were Kate's rocks made of one or more minerals?

Color is one property of rocks. Size is a property too. Very large rocks are called boulders. Some boulders may be larger than a car. Very small rocks may be as small as a dime. Where might you find boulders? Where might you find very small rocks?

Shape and texture are properties of rocks, too. Look at the shape of the rock below. Imagine how it would feel to touch the rocks. What do you think caused the rock to look like it does?

Activity

What Are Some Rocks Like?

What to use:

12 different rocks	masking tape
egg carton	marker
hand lens	pencil and paper

What to do:

1. Number your paper from 1 to 12.

2. Collect 12 rocks. Use the tape and pencil to number each rock.

3. On the paper, write where you found each rock next to its number.

4. Observe each rock. Record how it looks and feels.

What did you learn?

1. Which words are used most often to tell about the rocks?

2. How are the rocks alike?

3. How are the rocks different?

Using what you learned:

1. Choose a rock made of more than one mineral. How do you know if a rock is made of many minerals?

2. How can you tell if some of your rocks were the same kind?

Where Are Rocks Found?

When you slice an apple, you find different layers. A small core is in the center. A thick layer is in the middle. A thin skin is all around the outside. Scientists cannot slice the Earth. However, they know the Earth has layers, too. The Earth is made of a core in the center. It has a thick layer in the middle. Its thin top layer is around the outside. The Earth's top layer is called the **crust.** Find the crust in the picture below.

Most of the crust is made of very large areas of solid rock. Layers of soil cover these large rocks. In some places ice and snow may cover the rocks. In some places deep ocean water covers the rocks. The small rocks you see on the ground came from the larger rocks of the crust.

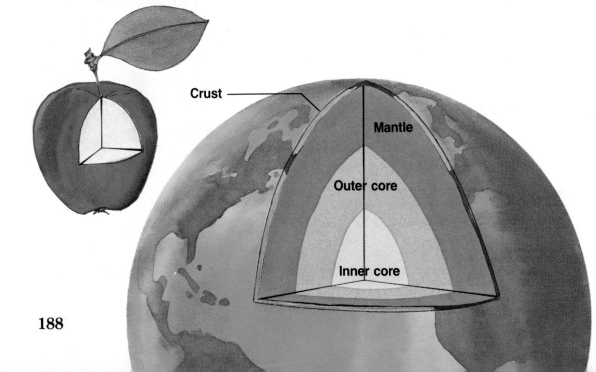

Crust

Mantle

Outer core

Inner core

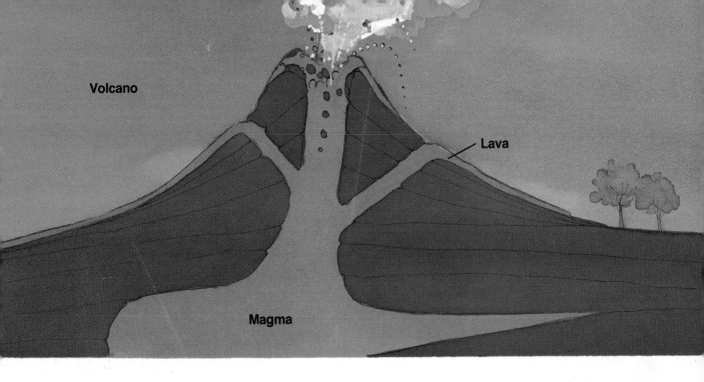

Volcano

Lava

Magma

Liquid Rock

Hot liquid rock is deep inside the crust. Hot liquid rock inside the crust is called **magma** (MAG muh). Magma is squeezed from place to place deep in the crust. Sometimes magma moves up through spaces between the large rock areas in the Earth's crust. The magma cools slowly as it moves closer to the Earth's surface. Magma changes to solid rock when it cools.

Sometimes magma flows onto the surface of the Earth. One place where magma flows to the surface of the Earth is called a volcano. Sometimes a lot of magma flows quickly out of a volcano. Magma that reaches the Earth's surface is called **lava.** Lava flows over the ground and cools quickly. Lava hardens to form rock when it cools.

Rocks that form from magma and lava are called **igneous** (IHG nee us) **rocks.** All igneous rocks do not look the same. The two rocks on top formed from lava. What different properties do the rocks have? The rocks on the left formed from magma. What different properties do these rocks have?

The rocks on this page have mineral pieces of different sizes. The size of minerals in igneous rocks shows where the rocks formed. You know that some rocks form from lava. Lava cools quickly. Large mineral pieces do not have time to form. So, rocks made from lava have small mineral pieces. Rocks also form from magma. Magma cools slowly. What is the size of minerals in rocks made from magma? Why do you think magma cools slower than lava?

Rocks from Rock Pieces

Large rocks can break into smaller rocks. The small rocks can break into very small rock pieces called **sediments** (SED uh munts). Sediments are small enough to be moved by water. Runoff carries the rock pieces into lakes and rivers. Once in the water, some of them drop to the bottom.

Some sediments are small enough to be moved by wind. Wind blows small pieces of rock and soil over land and water. When the wind slows down, the pieces drop to the Earth.

The sediments dropped in water and on land form layers. In hundreds of years, many layers form. The layers get very heavy. The top layers push down on the bottom layers. The bottom sediments are squeezed and packed together closely.

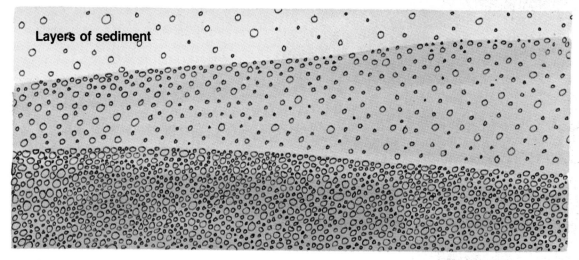

Layers of sediment

Water fills spaces around the sediments. The water evaporates. Minerals in the water are left in the spaces. The minerals glue the sediments together. The sediments are now rocks. Rocks made from sediments are called **sedimentary** (sed uh MENT uh ree) **rocks.** Which of these rocks was made from large sediments? Which was made from small sediments?

Dead plant or animal parts may be in some sediments. Shells, bones, and other parts are covered by soil, rock, and mud. Over a long time, these parts change to sedimentary rocks. Coal is made from plants that lived a long time ago.

Activity

How Is a Sedimentary Rock Made?

What to use:

paper cup   cementing solution
sand   hand lens

What to do:

1. Fill the paper cup half full of sand. Pack the sand with your hand.

2. Slowly add cementing solution until all of the sand is wet.

3. Put the cup in a warm place until the sand dries completely.

4. Carefully tear away the paper cup.

5. Observe the sand with the hand lens.

What did you learn?

1. How has the sand changed?
2. How is your rock like a sedimentary rock?

Using what you learned:

1. How is natural sandstone made?
2. Why is a cement sidewalk like a sedimentary rock?

Rocks Changed from Other Rocks

Look at these two rocks. Both rocks used to be the same. Now the bottom rock is changed. How has it changed?

Sometimes rocks are buried deep under the ground. Soil and other rocks above are very heavy. They press down on the underground rocks. The underground rocks are heated as the other rocks push down on them.

Rocks change when they are squeezed and heated. Rocks that are squeezed and heated change into **metamorphic** (met uh MOR fihk) **rocks.** Metamorphic rocks are very hard. Some metamorphic rocks have bands. The bands are made when the minerals are heated and squeezed. What metamorphic rock is found in the place shown below?

194

Activity

How Is Metamorphic Rock Made?

What to use:

wet pottery clay (3 kg)   10 paper clips
2 sheets waxed paper   heavy book

What to do:

1. Make 3 clay cakes 10 centimeters long on each side and 1 centimeter thick.

2. Push paper clips into all parts of the clay.

3. Stack the cakes on some waxed paper.

4. Put waxed paper on top of the stack. Lay a book on top of the stack. Press down hard on the book.

5. Remove the book and waxed paper.

6. Observe any changes in the stack.

What did you learn?

1. How did the clay cakes change when they were squeezed?

2. What happened to the paper clips?

Using what you learned:

1. How is the squeezed clay like a metamorphic rock?

2. What did you learn by observing what happened to the paper clips?

People and Science

Looking for Rocks

What do you think a rock hound is? It is not a rock. It is not a dog. A rock hound is a person who collects rocks.

Mark is a rock hound. He has more than 50 different rocks. Mark spends much time looking for rocks. He finds rocks in many places. He looks for rocks of all colors. He looks for rocks with strange shapes. Mark has one rock that looks like a dog's head.

Mark spends much time reading about rocks, too. He knows the names of many rocks. He also knows how the rocks were formed. Mark can tell you what minerals make up the rocks he finds.

You can become a rock hound, too. Maybe you will find some unusual rocks. What will you need to collect these rocks?

Chapter Review

Summary

- Minerals are nonliving solids found in the Earth.
- Rocks are made of minerals.
- The crust is the thin top layer of the Earth.
- Rocks are found in the Earth's crust.
- Igneous rocks form when magma or lava cools.
- Small pieces of broken rock are called sediments.
- Sedimentary rocks form when sediments are glued together.
- Rocks that are heated and squeezed are changed into metamorphic rocks.

Science Words

mineral	**igneous rocks**
crust	**sediments**
magma	**sedimentary rocks**
lava	**metamorphic rocks**

Questions

1. How are all rocks alike?
2. Why do some rocks have more than one color?
3. How is the Earth like an apple?
4. When does magma cool quickly?
5. How do igneous rocks form?
6. What carries sediments from place to place?
7. Which kind of rocks can be made from parts of plants and animals?
8. Where do metamorphic rocks form?

Chapter Two

Nature Changes Rocks

What kind of rocks are in this picture? How are the rocks changing? What is causing the change?

Rocks are changing. Wind, water, and living things change rocks. They break large rocks into smaller rocks. Sometimes, they wear away very small rock pieces. The breaking or wearing away of rocks is called **weathering.** Weathering is always taking place. Some weathering happens quickly. Some weathering happens slowly.

Water Changes Rocks

Water causes much weathering. It changes rocks in different ways. Fast moving water picks up sediments. The sediments hit other rocks. As they hit the rocks, the sediments chip off small pieces of the rocks. What happens to the surfaces of rocks that are in fast moving streams for many years?

Activity

What Breaks Rocks?

What to use:

plaster of paris   marking pen   water
small spoon   liquid soap   dish
small paper cup   freezer

What to do:

1. Put 5 spoonsful of plaster of paris in a paper cup. Add water to wet the mixture and stir.

2. Dip the marking pen in liquid soap. Push it into the center of the plaster.

3. After the plaster dries, remove the pen. Tear off the paper cup.

4. Fill the pen hole with water. Put the plaster mold on a dish and place it in a freezer for one day.

5. Remove the mold and dish from the freezer. Observe what happened.

What did you learn?

1. How has the water changed?
2. What happened to the plaster?

Using what you learned:

1. How can ice make holes in roads?
2. How can ice change rocks?

Rocks may have cracks in their surfaces. Water flows into the cracks. If the temperature is cold enough, the water will freeze. Water expands as it changes to ice. The ice pushes the cracks apart. Over the years, water in the cracks may melt and freeze many times. The cracks get bigger each time ice forms. Finally, the rocks break.

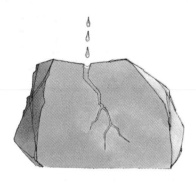

Sometimes water soaks into rocks. Minerals in the rocks mix with the water. The minerals are removed from the rocks when the water moves out. Holes are left where the minerals used to be. The rocks break apart.

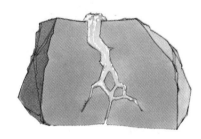

Water can break rocks into small pieces. Water can also cause the erosion (ih ROH zhun) of those rocks. **Erosion** is the moving of sediments to a new place. As rocks in streams break, water carries off the pieces. A slow moving stream moves only very small pieces of rock and soil. Fast streams can move larger pieces, too. Why is erosion greater in fast streams? What happens to the sediments when the water slows down?

Water erosion may happen on land. Floods can wash away both rocks and soil. Floods can move large rocks, trees, cars, and homes with fast-moving water.

Wind Changes Rocks

Wind can cause weathering and erosion. Wind can blow sediments against rocks. The rocks slowly wear away. Sometimes the wind carves rocks into strange shapes. How is the carving of rocks a type of weathering?

A dust storm is shown below. Dust storms cause weathering. Dust storms also cause erosion. Which would move larger pieces of rock—a dust storm or a flood? Which would move pieces of rocks faster—a dust storm or a flood?

Living Things Change Rocks

Plants can change rocks. Some plants need little soil to grow. These plants grow in the soil that fills the cracks in rocks. The roots and stems push on the rocks as they grow. They make the cracks larger. The rocks may break if the plants grow large enough.

Animals can change rocks, too. They make places for weathering to happen. They chip rocks as they dig for food and shelter. Some animals dig tunnels in the ground. They loosen the rocks and soil. Water and wind carry away the sediments.

Name two animals that help change rocks. What do the two animals do to change the rocks?

People change rocks, too. People use machines to break rocks. They carry rocks away in trucks. People dig tunnels and build roads through rocks.

How are people changing rocks here? How are they using the rocks? How do you use rocks?

New Rocks From Old

Nature changes rocks. As the rocks change, they become part of a cycle. One kind of rock changes to another kind of rock. The changing of rocks into other rocks is the **rock cycle.** The rock cycle never ends. All rocks are part of the cycle.

Igneous rocks are made from cooled magma and lava. Wind, water, and living things change igneous rocks. They change the rocks to sediments. The sediments may change to new rocks. What kind of rocks would the sediments make?

Some igneous rocks may be buried deep in the ground. The rocks are squeezed and heated. Igneous rocks become metamorphic rocks. Do you think these rocks change quickly or slowly?

Sometimes igneous rocks are buried very, very deep in the ground. The rocks are squeezed and heated so much that they melt. They become hot liquid rock again. What kind of rocks will form when the hot liquid rock cools?

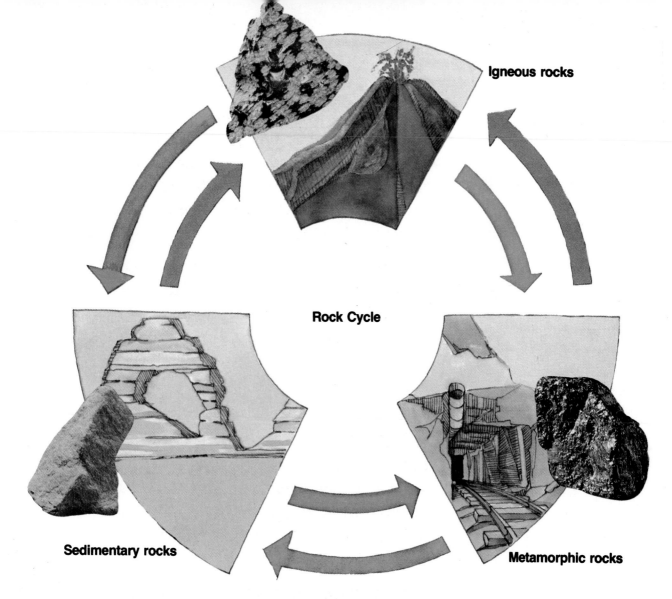

Igneous rocks

Rock Cycle

Sedimentary rocks

Metamorphic rocks

Wind, water, and living things change sedimentary and metamorphic rocks, too. Small pieces from these rocks become new sedimentary rocks. Sedimentary and metamorphic rocks can be buried, too. What happens to these rocks when they are squeezed and heated? How can these rocks change to igneous rocks?

The picture shows the rock cycle. Tell what the colored arrows mean.

Icicles Made of Stone

What looks like an icicle but is made of stone? A stalactite does. Stalactites hang from the roofs of caves. Some are so big that they touch the floor.

Stalactites take many years to form. Water and minerals seep through the ground. They form drops on the roof of a cave. The water may evaporate. Some of the minerals are left on the roof. A small, stone icicle begins to grow. Some of the water and minerals may also drop to the floor. The water evaporates. The minerals are left on the floor. The minerals form a stalagmite. Stalagmites may grow very tall.

Caves may have whole rooms full of stalactites and stalagmites. People even take tours of the caves. They give the rooms special names. One room is called The Grand Palace. What would you call the room in this cave?

Chapter Review

Summary

- Weathering breaks rocks into smaller pieces.
- Water weathers rocks in different ways.
- Erosion happens when sediments are carried to a new place.
- Water can cause erosion of sediments.
- Wind and living things can also cause the weathering and erosion of rocks.
- The changing of rocks from one kind to another is the rock cycle.
- The rock cycle is always happening.

Science Words

weathering
erosion
rock cycle

Questions

1. How is erosion different from weathering?
2. What three ways can water change rocks?
3. Compare the size of sediments carried by wind and water.
4. Name three living things that cause weathering and erosion. How do they change the rocks?
5. What is the rock cycle?
6. How can a metamorphic rock change into a sedimentary rock?

Unit 6 Review

 ## Self Checks

Answer these Self Checks on a sheet of paper.

1. Name the three kinds of rocks.
2. Tell how each kind of rock is formed.
3. Draw a picture of the rock cycle. Include the three kinds of rocks in the cycle.
4. What is causing the erosion of rocks in each picture?

5. Tell how these rocks change to the other rocks.
   (a) sedimentary to igneous
   (b) igneous to sedimentary
   (c) metamorphic to sedimentary
   (d) sedimentary to sedimentary
6. What kind of rock is made in each place?

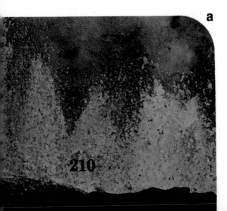

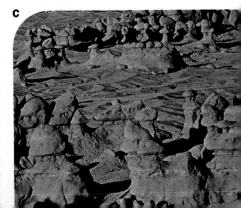

Idea Corner
More Fun with Science

1. Put a group of rocks on a table. Describe two properties of one rock. See whether the other students can find your rock.

2. Take a walk around your school yard. Find examples of rocks being changed.

3. Make a picture collection of rock erosion by
   (a) wind   (c) oceans
   (b) glaciers   (d) people

4. Ask a rock hound to visit your classroom. Ask the person to bring a rock collection.

5. Collect pictures of rocks that show interesting colors or shapes. Think of a good name for each rock. Show them to your class.

Reading for Fun

How to Dig a Hole to the Other Side of the World by Faith McNulty, Harper and Row Publishing Co.: New York, © 1979.

   What is the inner part of the Earth made of and how would you describe it?

Rock-Hound's Book by Seymour Simon, Penguin Books, Inc.: New York, © 1976.

   Learn all there is to know about finding rocks.

Rocks and Minerals by Robin Kerrod, Warwick Publishers: Oklahoma City, © 1977.

   How are rock and mineral deposits formed?

Unit 7

Chapter One

The Earth and Moon

What do you know about the moon? How is it like the Earth? How is it different?

People have been interested in the moon for thousands of years. They made up stories to explain the moon and its movements. People are still interested in the moon. Scientists know many things about the moon. They use these facts to compare the moon to the Earth.

Which Is Bigger?

The Earth looks small in the bottom picture. It looks even smaller than the moon. The moon is really smaller than the Earth. Look at the pictures on the right. They can help you understand why the Earth looks so small.

The purple and yellow balls are not the same size. Which ball is smaller? Look at the bottom picture. Which ball looks smaller? The large ball is farther away than the smaller ball. So, the large ball looks smaller than it really is. Objects look smaller as they get farther away. Why does the Earth look smaller than the moon?

Activity

How Large Are the Circles?

What to use:

cardboard   modeling clay   circle patterns
scissors   meter stick   long table

What to do:

1. Trace the circle patterns on the sheet of cardboard. Cut out the circles.

2. Put each circle in a piece of clay.

3. Put the smallest circle 60 cm from the table's edge. Put the middle-sized circle 90 cm from the table's edge. Put the largest circle 120 cm from the edge.

4. Kneel down at the table's edge. Close one eye. Look at all of the circles at the same time.

What did you learn?

1. Which circle was the closest to you?
2. Which circle was the farthest from you?
3. What size did all of the circles seem to be in step 4?

Using what you learned:

1. Why does the sun sometimes look the same size as the moon?
2. When can a real airplane look the same size as a toy plane?

Hills and Valleys

Size is one property scientists compare when they study the Earth and moon. They also compare the way each surface looks. Scientists have found that the surfaces are alike in some ways. They are also different in some ways.

Hills and mountains are found on the moon. Some mountains are very high. They are as tall as the mountains on Earth. Moon mountains are also very sharp and rough. Some Earth mountains are smooth. Weathering and erosion have worn down the sharp edges of these Earth mountains. What causes weathering and erosion on Earth? Why do you think weathering and erosion do not happen on the moon?

Moon mountains are made of bare rocks and "soil." Earth mountains are made of rocks and soil, too. Earth mountains also have trees, bushes, and other plants. Think about what plants need to grow. Why do plants not grow on the moon?

Both the Earth and moon have valleys. Long, narrow moon valleys are called **rills.** Some moon rills look like cracks in the surface. Some look like winding paths.

Most Earth valleys were formed by streams or rivers. Moving water cuts paths through soil and rocks. As time passed, the water cuts deeper and wider paths in the Earth's surface. Why do you think rills were not formed in the same way Earth valleys were formed?

Plains and Seas

Imagine that you are looking at the moon one night. You see dark areas on the moon's surface. These dark areas are very large, flat plains. Long ago, people thought these areas were filled with water. They called the dark areas seas. Scientists now know the moon's **seas** are plains made of dark rocks and dust. What fills the seas on Earth? Look at the picture above. Find the moon seas.

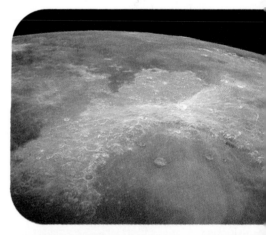

The Earth has plains, too. They are large, flat areas. Earth plains have thick, rich soil. People may grow crops in the rich soil. There are no plants growing on the moon. The moon soil is not thick and rich. Moon plains are very bare and dry.

Activity

How Can You Make Moon Craters?

What to use:

plastic dishpan
sand
large marble
string (1 1/2 meters)
masking tape

newspaper
baby powder
flashlight
metric ruler
pencil and paper

What to do:

Part A

1. Cover a square meter area with newspaper. Place the dishpan in the center of the paper.

2. Pour sand into the dishpan until it is 5 cm deep. Sprinkle a thin layer of baby powder on top of the sand.

3. Tape one end of the string to the marble.

4. Hold the other end of the string in one hand. With the other hand, hold the marble a little less than 1 meter above the pan.

5. Drop the marble into the sand. With the string, carefully lift the marble straight out of the sand.

6. Observe the crater in the sand.

7. Measure the size of the marble and the crater. Record your measurements.

Part B

1. Shine a flashlight straight down on the crater. Draw what you observe.

2. Shine the light on the crater from one side. Draw what you observe.

What did you learn?

1. What happened to the sand when the marble hit? How can you tell?
2. What is the shape of the crater?
3. What is the distance across the crater?
4. What is the distance across the marble?
5. What does the crater look like when you shine the flashlight straight down?
6. What does the crater look like when you shine the flashlight from one side?

Using what you learned:

1. How does the size of the marble compare to the size of the crater it makes?
2. Why did you put a layer of baby powder on top of the sand?
3. What does the marble represent?
4. What does the flashlight represent?
5. How can you use moon craters and the shadows in craters to find the direction of the sun?

Craters

Scientists think that a very long time ago the moon had volcanoes. There are no volcanoes on the moon now. There are some craters that may have been formed by volcanoes. A **crater** is a hole in the ground. The moon is covered with craters. Most moon craters were made by objects hitting the moon. What objects might hit the moon?

The Earth has craters, too. One crater is in the state of Arizona. This crater is like a moon crater. It was made by an object hitting the Earth.

Why do you think there are more craters on the moon than on the Earth? Why do Earth craters look different from moon craters after a long period of time?

Rocks and Soil

Scientists put all of the rocks on Earth into three groups. You have learned how these kinds of rocks form. Moon rocks are like some Earth rocks. Igneous rocks are found on the moon. Igneous rocks on Earth are made from cooled magma or lava. Scientists think that the igneous rocks on the moon were made the same way. Why do you think scientists probably will not find sedimentary rocks on the moon?

Soil on Earth is not all the same. Some Earth soil is wet and firmly packed. Some is dry and sandy. Most soil contains pieces of plant and animal parts. Leaves, twigs, bones, and shells are mixed in the top layer of soil.

Moon soil is like some dry sand found on Earth. The moon soil is made from small pieces of rock. No water or plant and animal parts have been found in any soil on the moon.

Surface Temperature

The temperature on Earth changes with the seasons. Some places are cold most of the year. Some places are warm all year. Many plants and animals in these places are adapted to the different types of temperatures. Many places on Earth have a few months of both kinds of temperature. Plants and animals in these places can adapt to the seasons.

The temperature on the moon changes very quickly. It changes very quickly with day and night. The moon is very hot where the sun shines on it. It is much hotter than any place on Earth. On the dark side, the moon is very cold. It is colder than any place on Earth. Plants and animals from Earth cannot live with the quick temperature changes found on the moon.

Gravity

You learned that gravity is a force. Gravity pulls you back to Earth if you jump into the air. The force of gravity can also be felt on the moon. However, the Earth has more gravity than the moon. The Earth's gravity is six times greater than the moon's. Because of gravity, you weigh six times more on Earth than you would on the moon.

More to Learn

Scientists have learned much about the moon. They know the moon is like the Earth in some ways. They know the moon is also very different. There is still much more to learn about the moon. Why do you think scientists want to learn more about the moon?

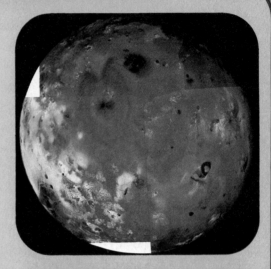

Many Moons

How many moons are there? The Earth has one moon. Some other planets have moons, too. Mars and Neptune have two moons. Jupiter may have more than fifteen moons.

All moons are not the same. They are many sizes. They are different shapes. They are not all made of the same things.

In 1979 the two Voyager spacecraft moved past Jupiter. Both spacecraft took pictures of the planet's moons. Scientists were surprised when they looked at the pictures. One of Jupiter's moons is called Io. The pictures showed that Io has active volcanoes. Io's volcanoes are more violent than any volcanoes on Earth. So far, Io and Earth are the only two places in space that scientists know have active volcanoes.

One of Jupiter's other moons is called Europa. Europa is about the same size as the Earth's moon. Its surface is covered with a thin layer of ice. Scientists think that water or slush is under the ice layer.

Scientists are trying to find out more about all of Jupiter's moons. Maybe someday astronauts will land on these moons, too.

Chapter Review

Summary

- The Earth is larger than the moon.
- Distance can make objects look smaller than they are.
- Both the Earth and moon have mountains, valleys, and plains.
- Weathering and erosion happen on Earth but not on the moon.
- Moon valleys are called rills.
- The moon has no water.
- The moon's seas are really plains of rocks and dust.
- Both the Earth and moon have craters.
- Igneous rocks are found on the Earth and moon.
- The moon gets colder and hotter than Earth.
- The Earth's gravity is six times greater than the moon's.

Science Words

rills   **seas**   **crater**

Questions

1. How does distance change the way objects look?
2. How are most moon craters formed?
3. Why can weathering and erosion happen on Earth and not on the moon?
4. How are Earth and moon mountains the same?
5. Which is bigger, the Earth or the moon?
6. Why could plants from Earth not live on the moon?
7. What happens to a person's weight on the moon?
8. What kind of rocks are on both the Earth and moon?

Chapter Two

Earth and Moon Movements

How do you know the Earth is moving?
How do you know the moon is moving?
Why does the moon seem to change shape?

Ｙou are at an exciting football game. You see the ball being thrown and caught. You see the players running. You stand up and cheer as your team wins the game. At the end of the game, you reach for your books. They should be right beside you. The books are not there. They are a few meters away, right where you put them down. What happened?

How Do You Know Objects Move?

Sometimes it is easy to know objects move. It was easy for you to see the ball and players move. It may be hard to know that other objects move. You did not see or feel yourself move away from your books.

Both the Earth and moon move. It is easy to think that the moon moves. You can watch the moon change its place in the night sky. It is not so easy to think that the Earth moves. You cannot watch the Earth change its place.

Two Natural Satellites

If you traveled out in space, you would see that the Earth and moon move. They both move around other objects in space. The Earth moves around the sun. The moon moves around the Earth. An object that moves around a larger object is called a **satellite** (SAT uh lite). The moon is a satellite of the Earth. What is the sun's satellite? What are some other satellites you can name?

Scientists always know where the moon is in space. The moon follows a path around the Earth. The path is called an orbit. A satellite follows an **orbit** or path around another object. The Earth has an orbit. Where is the Earth's orbit?

The moon is a natural satellite of the Earth. The moon was not made by people. The Earth has other satellites, too. These satellites are machines made by people. They are used by people to learn more about space and the Earth. What might people learn about the Earth from these satellites?

Two Movements in Space

The moving train is going around the girl. It is revolving. **Revolving** means that one object goes around another object. The revolving object follows an orbit as it moves. Our moon revolves in an orbit around the Earth. The moon takes about 28 days to revolve around the Earth.

The Earth is revolving, too. It follows an orbit around the sun. The Earth follows a larger orbit than the moon. So, the Earth takes a longer time to revolve. It takes the Earth one year to revolve around the sun.

What is this man doing? How is the ball moving? Scientists would say the ball is rotating (ROH tay ting). **Rotating** means that an object spins. The ball rotates one time when it makes one complete spin.

Just as the ball rotates, the Earth and moon rotate. The Earth rotates one time every 24 hours. What other name do we use when we speak of 24 hours?

The moon does not rotate as fast as the Earth. The moon takes about 28 days to rotate one time. What other movement does the moon make that takes about the same amount of time?

Activity

What Is Moonlight?

What to use:

flashlight   mirror   globe   meter stick

What to do:

1. Work with two other students. Stand in a triangle with sides 2 meters long.

2. Have each student stand at a different corner of the triangle. Student A holds the flashlight, B holds the globe, and C holds the mirror.

3. Turn out the lights. Observe the globe.

4. Turn on the flashlight and shine the light on the mirror. Hold the mirror so the light is reflected to the globe.

What did you learn?

1. What did you observe about the mirror and the globe before and after the flashlight was turned on?

2. Where does moonlight come from?

Using what you learned:

1. What do the flashlight, globe, and mirror represent?

2. Where does the moonlight we see on Earth come from?

Moon Phases

The moon does not make its own light. Moonlight is really sunlight. Light from the sun shines on the moon. The light bounces off the moon and shines on the Earth. We see this light from Earth. We call the light moonlight.

Half of the moon's surface is always facing the sun. The part facing the sun gets sunlight. The half facing away from the sun is dark. Sometimes you can see the whole lighted side of the moon. At other times, we can see only part of the lighted side. The amount of the lighted side that you see changes from night to night. The lighted part of the moon that you see from Earth is called a **phase** (FAYZ). You can see different moon phases from Earth. Which of these phases have you seen?

Activity

What Are Moon Phases?

What to use:

flashlight   white softball
globe   pencil and paper

What to do:

1. Work with two other students. Hold the globe so your country faces the student holding the flashlight.

2. Have the third student hold the ball between the globe and flashlight.

3. Turn out the lights and turn on the flashlight. Draw a picture of how much of the lighted side of the ball you see from the globe. Label your drawing A.

4. Move the ball to each place shown. Draw and label the shapes you see.

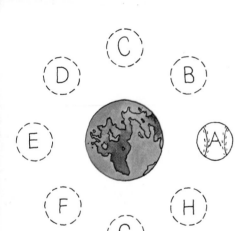

What did you learn?

1. How much light does the ball always get?
2. How did the lighted shapes you saw change as the ball was moved?

Using what you learned:

1. What do the flashlight, ball, and globe each stand for?
2. The moon takes about 28 days to revolve around the Earth. What happens after that?

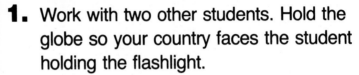

Waxing moon

Waning moon

Moon phases change in a cycle. The cycle lasts for about 29 1/2 days. The moon's cycle begins with the new moon phase. During the **new moon,** all of the lighted side faces away from the Earth. You cannot see the new moon. You see a small part of the moon on the next night. Each night you see more. People say the moon is waxing. A **waxing** moon has more of its lighted side showing each night.

You see all of the lighted side of the moon during the **full moon** phase. The full moon happens halfway through the phase cycle. You see less of the moon each night after the full moon. People say the moon is waning. A **waning** moon has less of its lighted side showing each night.

People have names for the shapes of the moon during its cycle. Full moon and new moon are two of eight moon phases. Look at the next page. It shows how the eight phases look. All eight phases repeat again and again.

The moon does not really change shape. You see phases because both the Earth and moon are moving. Both rotate. Both revolve. What do you think would happen if the moon did not revolve?

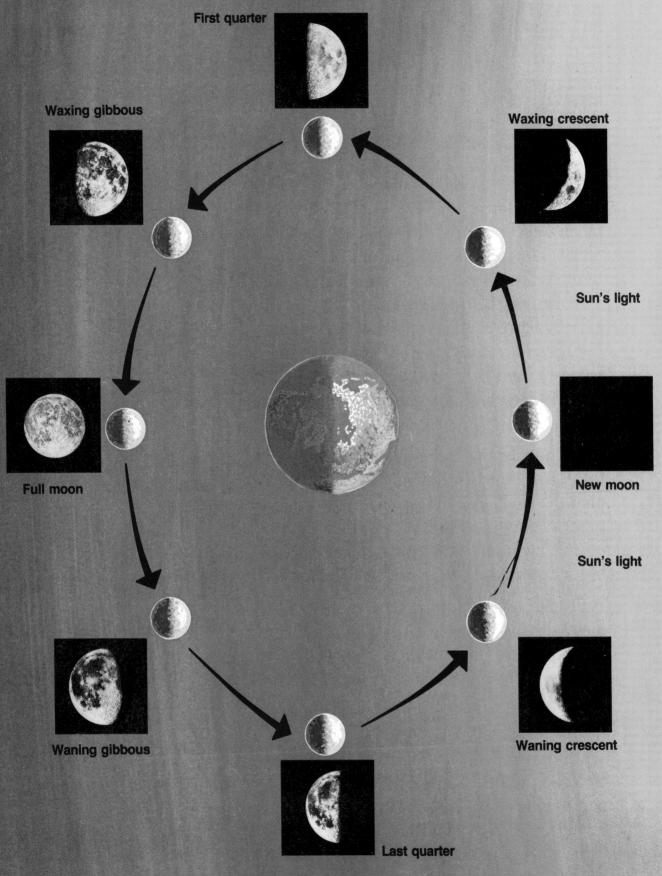

First quarter

Waxing gibbous

Waxing crescent

Sun's light

Full moon

New moon

Waning gibbous

Sun's light

Waning crescent

Last quarter

Chapter Review

Summary

- Both the Earth and moon are satellites.
- All satellites follow an orbit around another object.
- The moon revolves around the Earth. The Earth revolves around the sun.
- Both the Earth and moon rotate.
- Moonlight is really sunlight.
- The part of the moon you see from the Earth is called a phase.
- Moon phases are part of a cycle that never ends.

Science Words

satellite	new moon
orbit	waxing
revolving	full moon
rotating	waning
phase	

Questions

1. Why is the moon called a satellite?
2. List two objects besides the Earth and moon that revolve.
3. List two objects besides the Earth and moon that rotate.
4. Why can you see light from the moon?
5. How many full moons can you see in a month?
6. Why can you not see the new moon?
7. Why do people see moon phases?
8. Explain what is meant by a waning moon.

Chapter Three

How Scientists Learn About the Moon

Why do scientists want to learn more about the moon? What tools do they use to observe the moon?

How often have you looked at the moon? Most people use only their eyes when they observe the moon. They cannot see the moon's mountains, valleys, seas, and craters. They see only light and dark areas on the moon's surface. Scientists use special equipment to observe the moon.

Observing the Moon from Earth

This student is using a telescope. A **telescope** is a tool used to make faraway objects look bigger. The bottom picture shows how the moon looks through some telescopes. Compare the way the moon looks in both pictures. Which picture is better for studying the moon?

241

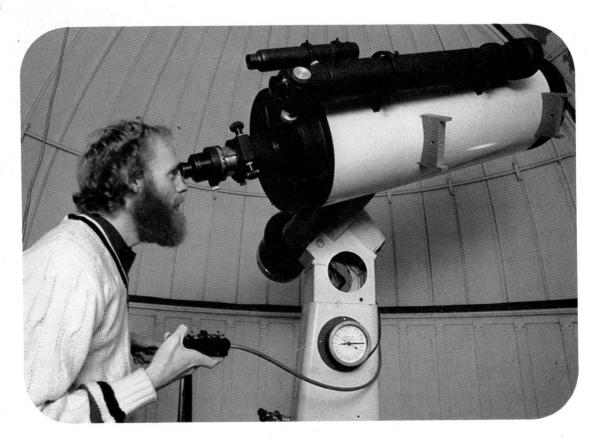

Scientists use larger telescopes than the girl has. Larger telescopes make the moon look even bigger. Scientists can learn more about the moon's surface when they use the larger telescopes. They can see where valleys cut through tall mountains. They can see small craters inside large craters. The scientists are able to make maps of the moon. Why would they want a map of the moon?

Scientists also see that the hills, valleys, seas, and craters do not change. They stay the same size and shape. Weathering and erosion do not happen. Since weathering and erosion do not happen, scientists know there is no water or wind on the moon.

Observing the Moon from Space

Scientists have other ways to observe the moon. They use spacecraft. **Spacecraft** are machines that travel from the Earth to the moon or other space objects. Most spacecraft do not carry people. Scientists on Earth control where the spacecraft go. They control what information the spacecraft collect. Some spacecraft orbit the moon and return to Earth. Some land on the moon.

A few spacecraft have carried people to the moon. People who travel and work in space are **astronauts** (AS truh nawts). Astronauts have learned a lot about the moon. They have collected moon rocks and soil. They have walked on the moon's surface. They found out how it feels to live in a place that has less gravity than Earth. Why would people want to go to the moon?

Tools Astronauts Use

People need special clothing to live on the moon. Clothing protects the astronauts when they are out of their spacecraft. The cloth used must be strong. It must not tear easily. The cloth must be able to protect the astronauts from very hot and cold temperatures.

Astronauts must carry their own air. Tanks of oxygen are hooked to their clothes. The astronauts carry these tanks on their backs when they go out of the spacecraft.

While on the moon's surface, astronauts use other special tools. One tool is the lunar rover. The rover is a machine that can be driven over the moon's surface. It is a moon car. Astronauts can explore the moon while riding in the rover.

How do you drink water? How do you prepare food? Astronauts store and prepare their water and food in special ways. The water and food are stored in small packages. Spacecraft are not very big. There is not much space for refrigerators, stoves, and fresh food. Some food the astronauts eat is shown here. Why do you think each food is in its own package? Why are the packages attached to the tray?

The astronaut above is drinking water. He is using a squeeze bottle. The bottle squirts liquid into his mouth. Why can the astronaut not use a glass like you do on Earth? What would happen if the astronaut tried to drink water from a glass while traveling through space?

People and Science

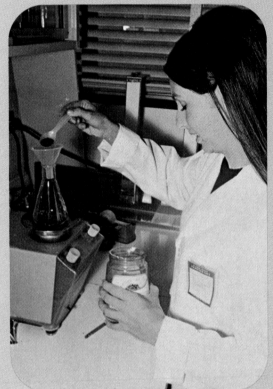

Food for the Astronauts

What kind of food is eaten in space? Astronauts need food that keeps them healthy. It must have many vitamins and minerals. The food must give the astronauts a lot of energy. All of the food must be easy to store. It must also look and taste good. Different kinds of foods must be used for each meal.

Food technicians prepare foods used by astronauts. Deanne is a food technician. She tests ways to store food. She also tests ways to prepare the food in space.

Deanne uses some freeze dried foods. Freeze dried food has most of the water removed. The water is removed when the food is very cold. Freeze dried foods are easy to store. They do not spoil quickly. During a flight, the astronauts add hot or cold water to the food. In about five minutes the food is ready to eat. It looks, smells, and tastes like food cooked on Earth.

Deanne likes her job. She knows the astronauts are eating good meals in space.

Chapter Review

Summary

- Telescopes make objects look bigger.
- Scientists use telescopes to observe the moon.
- Scientists use spacecraft to learn more about the moon.
- Some astronauts have gone to the moon.
- Astronauts have collected moon rocks and soil.
- People on the moon must have special clothes, air, food, and water to live.

Science Words

telescope
spacecraft
astronauts

Questions

1. What tool do scientists use to travel to the moon?
2. What tool do astronauts use to travel on the moon?
3. Why do scientists use telescopes to study the moon?
4. Why are air tanks important to astronauts as they walk on the moon?
5. Why can astronauts not prepare and store their food like people on Earth?
6. Why is it easier for scientists to study the moon from spacecraft than from Earth?

✓ Self Checks

Answer these Self Checks on a sheet of paper.

1. Which picture looks like the moon's surface? Why?

a

b

c

2. Which of these objects are rotating? Which are revolving?

d

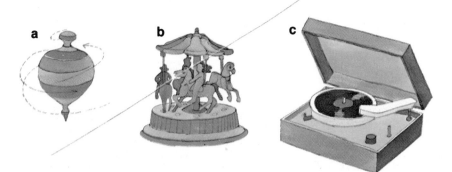

a   b   c

3. How are Earth and moon mountains different?

4. What is a satellite?

5. Why can we say moon phases change in a cycle?

6. What equipment does an astronaut need to live on the moon? Why is each type of equipment needed?

Idea Corner

More Fun with Science

1. Invite a person who has a telescope to bring it to class. Find out how it works. Have an evening moon party. Use the telescope to observe the moon.
2. Take a field trip to a planetarium or an observatory. Find out the difference between these two places.
3. Write a play about a trip to the moon. Present it to the rest of the class.
4. Make your own astronaut suit using materials around your home or school. Tell the class how your suit would protect you on the moon.

Reading for Fun

A Close Look at The Moon by G. Jeffrey Taylor, Dodd, Mead & Co.: New York, © 1980.

Study about the astronomy and geology of the moon.

The First Travel Guide to the Moon: What to Pack, How to Go, and What to See When You Get There by Rhoda Blumberg, Four Winds Press: Bristol, FL, © 1980.

Take a trip to the moon.

True Book of Spinoffs from Space by Leila Boyle Gemme, Children's Press, Inc.: Chicago, © 1977.

Many of the things we eat and use were first used in space.

Glossary

This book has words that you may not have read before, Many of these words are science words. Some science words may be hard for you to read. You will find the science words in **bold print**. These words may appear two ways. The first way shows how the word is spelled. The second way shows how the word

sounds. The list below shows the sounds each letter or group of letters makes.

Look at the word **energy** (EN ur gee). The second spelling shows the letters "ee." Find these letters in the list. The "ee" has the sound of "ea" in the word "leaf." Anytime you see "ee," you know what sound to say.

a . . . back (BAK)
er . . . care, fair (KER, FER)
ay . . . day (DAY)
ah . . . father (FAHTH ur)
ar . . . car (KAR)
ow . . . flower, loud (FLOW ur, LOWD)
e . . . less (LES)
ee . . . leaf (LEEF)
ih . . . trip (TRIHP)
i(i+con+e) . . .
   idea, life (i DEE uh, LIFE)
oh . . . go (GOH)
aw . . . soft (SAWFT)
or . . . orbit (OR but)
oy . . . coin (KOYN)

oo . . . foot (FOOT)
yoo . . . pure (PYOOR)
ew . . . food (FEWD)
yew . . . few (FYEW)
uh(u+con) . . .
   comma, mother (KAHM uh, MUTH ur)
sh . . . shelf (SHELF)
ch . . . nature (NAY chur)
g . . . gift (GIHFT)
j . . . gem, edge (JEM, EJ)
ing . . . sing (SING)
zh . . . vision (VIHZH un)
k . . . cake (KAYK)
s . . . seed, cent (SEED, SENT)
z . . . zone, raise (ZOHN, RAYZ)

A

adapted (uh DAPT tud): a living thing that fits into its habitat

astronauts (AS truh nauts): people who travel and work in space

atoms: small parts of matter

C

Celsius (SEL see us): a scale used to measure temperature

clouds: object formed when water drops or crystals stick to dust in the air

compound leaves: leaves made of leaflets

compound machine: machine made of two or more simple machines

condense (kun DENS): a gas as it changes to a liquid

cones: part of some plants in which seeds form

conserve: to use wisely

consumer: a living thing that must eat other living things for food

contracts (kun TRAKTS): matter that gets smaller and takes up less space

crater: a hole in the ground

crust: the Earth's top layer

D

desert: a place that does not have much rain

dew: a form of condensation

E

embryo (EM bree oh): tiny plant inside a seed

energy (EN ur gee): the ability to do work

erosion (ih ROH zhun): the moving of sediments to a new place

evaporates (ih VAP uh rayts): a liquid as it changes to a gas

expands (ihk SPANDZ): matter that gets bigger and takes up more space

F

factory: a place that has many machines which are used to make one type of object

flower: part of some plants in which seeds form

fog: a cloud very close to the ground

food chains: plants, animals which eat the plants, and animals which eat other animals form food chains.

force: a push or a pull; push or pull that moves a lever

freeze: a liquid as it changes to a solid

frost: ice crystals that form on objects

fulcrum: point where a lever rocks back and forth

full moon: phase of the moon which has all of the lighted side facing Earth

G

gas: a state of matter that has no shape or size of its own

gear: a wheel with teeth

germinate: the growth of the embryo from a seed

glacier (GLAY shur): large river of ice

gram: unit used to measure mass

grassland: a place where most of the plants are grasses

gravity (GRAV ut ee): the pull between the Earth and other objects

green leaves: plant part where food is made

groundwater: water that soaks into the ground

H

habitat (HAB uh tat): a place where a plant or animal lives

I

icebergs: large blocks of floating glacier ice

igneous (IHG nee us) **rocks:** rocks formed from magma or lava

inclined plane: simple machine used to move objects to a higher place

K

kilogram (KIHL uh gram): 1000 grams

L

lava: magma that reaches the Earth's surface

leaflets: parts of a compound leaf

lever: simple machine which can be used to lift objects

liquid: state of matter that has a certain size but does not have a shape of its own

load: object lifted by a lever

M

magma (MAG muh): hot liquid rock inside the Earth's crust

mass: how much there is of an object

matter: object that takes up space and has mass

melt: a solid as it changes to a liquid

metamorphic (met uh MOR fihk) **rocks:** rocks formed from other rocks that are heated and squeezed

mineral (MIHN uh rul): a nonliving solid found as part of the Earth

N

need: anything a plant or animal must have to stay alive

new moon: moon phase in which all of the lighted side faces away from Earth

O

orbit: the path a satellite follows around an object

P

phase: the part of the moon you see from Earth

plant cycle: the germinating, growing, and forming of new seeds.

plant eaters: animals that eat plants or plant parts

pods: plant part of some plants in which seeds grow

polar areas: cold places near the North and South Poles

precipitation (prih sihp uh TAY shun): water that falls from clouds to the ground

predator (PRED ut ur): animal that hunts and eats other animals

prey: animals eaten by predators

producer (pruh DEW sur): a living thing that makes its own food

property (PRAHP urt ee): describes how an object looks, feels, or acts.

pulley: a simple machine used to lift heavy loads

R

rain forests: a hot and wet habitat

reservoir (REZ uv wor): a place that stores water

revolving: the movement of an object as it goes around another object

rills: long, narrow moon valleys

rock cycle: the changing of rocks into other rocks

roots: plant part which holds the plant in the ground and absorbs water from the ground

rotating: the movement of a spinning object

runoff: water that flows across the ground

S

satellite (SAT ul ite): an object that moves around a larger object

scattered: seeds being moved to other places

screw: an inclined plane wrapped around a post

seas: moon plains made of dark rocks and dust

sedimentary (sed uh MENT uh ree) **rocks:** rocks made from sediments

sediments (SED uh munts): very small rock pieces

seed: a tiny plant and stored food

seed coat: the tough skin of a seed

seedling: a young plant

seed plants: plants that grow from seeds

shelter: a place or object that protects plants or animals

simple leaves: broad, flat leaves with only one part

simple machines: machines with few or no moving parts

solid: state of matter that has a certain size and shape

spacecraft: machines that travel around the Earth, moon, or other space objects

state: a group of matter such as the solid state, the liquid state, and the gas state

stems: part of the plant which holds other plant parts above the ground

stored food: food in a seed for the embryo

T

telescope: tool used to make far away objects look bigger

temperate (TEM prut) **forest:** a forest habitat that has four seasons

transportation: machines used to carry people and objects

V

volcano: one place where magma flows onto the surface of the Earth

W

waning: phases of the moon which have less of the lighted side showing each night

water cycle: the evaporation, condensation, precipitation, and storage of all water on Earth

water vapor: water in the gas state

waxing: phases of the moon which have more of the lighted side showing each night

weathering: the breaking or wearing away of rocks

wedge (WEJ): simple machine made of two inclined planes

wheel and axle: a simple machine with a wheel that turns on a post

work: what is done when a force moves an object

Index

PHOTO CREDITS

3 4 5 6 7 8 9 10 11 12 13 14 15 — 89 88 87 86 85 84 83